LIFE 2: THE SEQUEL

WHAT HAPPENS WHEN YOU DIE?

ALEC MOTYER

TRUTHFOR**LIFE**

CHRISTIAN
FOCUS

Note on Bible Translations and Cross references

It is not possible, for length's sake, to quote every relevant portion of Scripture. Where cross references are given, please take time to look the passage up.

Most of the Scripture quotations are taken from the *Holy Bible, New International Version*. Copyright © 1973, 1978, 1984 by International Bible Society. Used by permission of Hodder & Stoughton Publishers, A member of the Hodder Headline Group. All rights reserved. 'NIV' is a registered trademark of International Bible Society. UK trademark number 1448790. Where this is inexact or not literal enough other renderings are offered.

KJV is the *King James Version*

NKJV is the *New King James Version*, Copyright © 1982 by Thomas Nelson, Inc. Used by permission. All rights reserved.

RV is the *Revised Version*

RSV is the *Revised Standard Version*, copyright 1952 [2nd edition, 1971] by the Division of Christian Education of the National Council of the Churches of Christ in the United States of America. Used by permission. All rights reserved.

NRSV is the *New Revised Standard Version*, copyright 1989, Division of Christian Education of the National Council of the Churches of Christ in the United States of America. Used by permission. All rights reserved.

ESV is the *English Standard Version*, copyright © 2001 by Crossway Bibles, a division of Good News Publishers. Used by permission. All rights reserved.

© Alec Motyer

ISBN 978-1-84550-343-7

10 9 8 7 6 5 4 3 2 1

First published in 1964
Revised edition published in 1996
entitled *After Death*
Reprinted in 2008 and 2013
by
Christian Focus Publications,
Geanies House, Fearn, Tain,
Ross-shire, IV20 1TW, Great Britain

www.christianfocus.com

Cover Design by Paul Lewis
Printed and Bound in USA

LIFE 2: THE SEQUEL

WHAT HAPPENS WHEN YOU DIE?

A most readable book and is accessible even to those who may not be habitual readers ... This is a book to read and re-read. It is worth its weight in gold ... a must for every library!

David Ellis
Evangelicals Now, Surrey, England

Nowadays the subject of death is not one for polite conversation. In my youth older folk in my family could often be overheard asking each other, 'Where would you like to be buried?' But even then the more important unasked query was, 'Where d'you think you'll go when you die?' This is the vital question that confronts us all, and in this book Alec Motyer provides an excellent guide to finding the answer.

Owen Thomas
Churchman Magazine, Watford, England

Contents

In Memoriam

Joyce Caine
Clare Barnard Hankey
Clodagh Hayward
James Holland
George Hopper
James Edward Whild
who entered glory while this book was in preparation
and many others, family and friends
who are also part of my treasure in heaven.

PREFACE

What is the point of such a small book on such a large subject?

It was with this same question that the preface to the 1964 edition of *After Death* began and, if it was appropriate then, how much more when substantially the same book rises from the dead thirty years later?

Well, for one thing, the topic has not gone away. People still want to know about 'after death'; they still need to be rescued from guesses, assumptions and falsehoods. And, secondly, there is, after all, no more important problem to be faced and answered. The cynic had a real point when he countered the question 'Is there a life after death?' with 'Is there a life before death?' It is not an improper rejoinder and is one which the Christian, open Bible in hand, must face and answer. Yet what is even our longest span on earth compared with eternity – or, as the Lord Jesus Himself said, what profit is it to gain the world and lose the soul?

The original book was a contribution to the *Christian Foundations Series* promoted by the Evangelical Fellowship of the Anglican Communion and published by Hodder and Stoughton. In that series, Conservative Evangelicals in the Church of England addressed themselves in the first instance to their own denomination. In this refurbished edition of *After Death* the same denominational orientation is sometimes evident – not now, however, as part of what Dr John Stott then spoke of as crusading into Anglicanism to reform it, but because sometimes the Anglican application remains the easiest way to make and illustrate a significant point.

I am grateful to Christian Focus Publications and Mr Malcolm Maclean for opening this door of opportunity for me. I have tried to enter it with an ambition that has not varied for the last fifty years and more, to discover and explain what the Bible teaches. My understanding of some matters conflicts with that of respected, beloved and far more able fellow-students of God's Word, but this, of course, is part of the excitement, even fun, of being under the authority of this great and holy book. After all, inspiration belongs to the Scriptures, not to our poor efforts to explain and understand. Therefore, where differences arise they are to be expressed with humility, and love must prevail within the unity of the Spirit in the bond of Him who is our peace, Jesus Christ our Lord.

Alec Motyer,
Bishopsteignton, 1995

1

THE LOVE THAT DREW SALVATION'S PLAN

To Christians the love of God is a reason for confidence in relation to death and the life to come. We face death with equanimity and hope – a joyful, expectant, sure hope – because we have come to know that not even death can separate us from the love of God (Rom. 8:38-39), and this love has been so perfectly proved that we can go forward fearlessly, for He who has loved us loves us still, and always will love us. Therefore we are secure.

'God is love'
But can this confidence be limited to Christians? If it is true that 'God is love' (1 John 4:8), and that 'God so loved the world' (John 3:16), then must we not say that this same security is the guaranteed inheritance of all, whether they lived before or after Christ, whether they knew the gospel or did not know it, whether they accepted or rejected Jesus? If God is almighty as well as love, then are not all alike safe, and does not an eternity of bliss lie beyond the grave for everyone?

Now these are vital issues. The discussion on which we are starting is no remote research project but a matter of intimate personal concern. We all face death; we all desire certainty that it will be well with us. We must therefore be sure beyond any doubt that we are thinking correctly about the love of God. In what way does He loves us? Does He love us all alike? Where is His love to be found? Is His love 'strong as death' (Song 8:6)

The Father and the Son

The first truth about the love of God to notice is this: that love is the relationship which exists between the Father and the Son within the Holy Trinity (John 3:35; 5:20; 10:17; 14:31; 15:9; 17:23, 24, 26). 'The Father loves the Son,' said the Lord Jesus Christ (John 3:35). The terms He used here are important. On other occasions He used such expressions as 'the Father has loved me' (John 15:9), but in the verse quoted He spoke individually of 'the Father' and 'the Son' – the first and second Persons of the Trinity. On another occasion too He taught of the relationship between the Father and Himself in their eternal or heavenly life by saying 'because you loved me before the creation of the world' (John 17:24).

This is by far the most important thing that we could understand about the love of God. It is indeed, the essence of the meaning of the famous 'God is love' quoted above. For we learn here that love is not some passing fancy on God's part, some light emotion here today and gone tomorrow. It is part and parcel of the very nature of God Himself, existing from all eternity between the Father and the Son.

Holy love
To say that love is the relation between Persons of the Trinity is to say that love belongs to the *character* of God.

It is not, however any old *sort* of love; it is only that sort of love which someone like God can display. Sometimes when we think of other people we remark, 'I never thought she (or he) would be attracted to someone like that.' We recognize that love goes hand in hand with character and are surprised to discover that the object of a person's love is a bit at variance with the character which – rightly or wrongly – we previously judged that person to have. In the same way, the love of God is anchored in His character. He can love only in ways suitable to the sort of Person He is.

We need not be surprised, therefore, that the Bible teaches that His love is holy and righteous. 'The Lord is righteous; he loves righteousness' (Ps. 11:7, lit.). What this verse expressed in abstract terms, the Bible also says in personal terms: 'The Lord loves the righteous' (Ps. 146:8). There is thus a moral strictness about the love of God. It must not be presumed upon and, indeed, it has an opposite which also is found in God and reserved for the wicked. Here is a truth which cannot be trifled with. Hosea recorded God's reaction to the people of his day in this way:

> Because of all their wickedness in Gilgal,
> I hated them there.
> Because of their sinful deeds
> I will drive them out of my house.
> I will no longer love them (Hosea 9:15).

The People of God: chosen, saved, kept
The most constant thing the Bible teaches about God's love, however, is that it is bestowed on those He regards as His own. In both Testaments, God is gathering a people who are specially His. In the Old Testament it was found within the nation of Israel (Deut. 4:37; Isa. 8:11-20). In the New Testament it is the 'Israel of God', the children of

Abraham by faith, all who belong to the Lord Jesus Christ (John 16:27; Rom. 4:16; Gal. 3:7, 26; 6:16). These are the recipients of His love, and He has shown and shows His love for them in three ways: first, in choosing them to be His own; secondly, in saving them for Himself; and thirdly, in protecting and preserving them. We must consider each of these in turn.

Selectivity

There is a selectivity in the love of God which the Bible often states but never explains. It even risks arguing in a circle! In an attempt to explain Israel's favoured position as the people of God, Deuteronomy appeals to the fact of God's love in choosing them. But it speaks in this way: 'The LORD did not set his affection on you and choose you because you were more numerous than other peoples, for you were the fewest of all peoples: but it was because the LORD loved you' (7:7). The negative side of the relationship implied in this verse is plain enough: it was not for any feature of the nation itself that it was chosen: it exerted no pressure upon God's free choice. But positively, why did God choose Israel? The answer is, because of His love for them. But why did He love them? Because He loved them.

The same is true of the New Testament. We can hear the wondering praise in John's invitation to see 'How great is the love the Father lavished on us, that we should be called children of God. And that is what we are! ... the world does not know us' (1 John 3:1). The fact of the existence of a distinct people of God is plain in this verse. We are seen over against 'the world' but we have been constituted into a distinct people by the unexplained fact that God loves us.

This is not to say that God's love is arbitrary, like human favouritism. His love grows out of His character and that character is perfectly good, perfectly holy. There is no blemish in it. God bestows His love in ways that are absolutely right in His infallible judgment. He has not thought fit to tell us on what grounds He chooses His people, but we may be assured that they are righteous and good grounds, consistent with His character. All we are told, however, is that He loves us because He loves us.

God's saving love
The second aspect of God's love for His people is salvation: 'in his love and in his mercy he redeemed them' (Isa. 63:9; see also Hosea 11:4; John 3:16; Rom. 5:5; 2 Cor. 5:14; Eph. 2:4; 5:2; 1 John 3:16; 4:9f.). Isaiah spoke these words about the Exodus of Israel from Egypt, an event which displays the selective application of saving love. Alone of the two nations in the land of Egypt, Israel was saved. And over and over again the Bible asserts the saving love of God for His people. Paul rejoices in (lit.) 'the great love wherewith he loved us' so that even 'when we were dead in transgressions' He 'made us alive with Christ' (Eph. 2:4, 5). For John it is this saving action which alone qualifies as a definition of God's love. He would insist that if we say that 'God is love' we must at once define our terms for 'this is love, not that we loved God but that he loved us, and sent his Son to be the propitiation for our sins' (1 John 4:8-10).

Protection, preservation
God's love also preserves His people. It is His changeless attitude towards them (Jer. 31:3), the motive for His parental correction of them (Prov. 3:12; Heb. 12:6), the explanation of His goodness (Isa. 38:17), the reason for their strength (Rom. 8:37), and the ground of their certainty of God's fatherly care (John 16:27).

The parental note is strong in the references to God's watchful love over His people, and it is understandable that it should be so. We are taught that the choosing of His people was the work of the Father (Eph. 1:3, 4), and that the grace of the Lord Jesus – that is, His saving grace – brings us into the experience of the love of God the Father (2 Cor. 13:14). Christian experience is precisely that of a son/child (John 1:12), or family member (Eph. 2:19), and God cares for His own as a loving Father (Matt. 10:29-31).

Universal love

But what of God's love for the world, for humankind? Are we not in danger of losing the general in the particular?

There is a sense in which it is proper to speak of God's universal love, and that is when, as Creator of all, He displays equal benevolence towards all, making the sun to shine on evil as well as good, and sending rain on the just and unjust alike (Matt. 5:45).

True enough: but this is a great deal less intimate than the detailed love whereby He chose, saved and keeps His own. The question is, therefore, whether love of this sort can be said to exist between God and the world? But the Bible's answer is clear: the love of God in its characteristic sense is not said to be the mode of His relationship with the world in such a way that everybody automatically, by virtue of human birth, experiences it in full flavour.

This sounds so harsh that clear thinking is necessary to come to grips with it. Firstly, let us say that while God looks with fatherly regard upon all His creatures (His general benevolence to all), He is not to be considered as Father to all alike in the particular sense in which His Fatherhood is affirmed for those who believe in Jesus. John makes this clear by using the phrase 'to become the sons of God' (John 1:12). For the very idea of 'becoming' a son involves first a state of 'not being' a son. This leads us to recall that the love of God is centred in the Lord

14

Jesus Christ. He is the chief object of the Father's love, the 'beloved Son in whom I am well pleased' (Matt. 3:17); Jesus is also the chief display of the Father's love, for 'he loved us and sent His Son to be the propitiation for our sins' (1 John 4:10). He is, furthermore, the sole passport to the Father's love, for 'he who loves me will be loved by my Father' and 'no-one comes to the Father except through me' (John 14:6).

Love on offer

Thus we can come back to the question: does God love the world? Certainly! Enough to send His Son to be the Saviour of the world (1 John 4:14)! But this means that the love of God for the world is something that is 'on offer', and not something universally, automatically and inevitably enjoyed. It is not like the safety net spread out under every trapeze artist. It is rather the blanket held by the fire-brigade, inviting the individual to jump. The verse which famously states the love of God for the world goes on first to define that love as an incredible saving action, the expenditure of the life of an only Son, and then to lay down a condition of enjoyment: 'For God so loved the world that he gave his one and only Son, that whoever believes in him shall not perish but have eternal life' (John 3:16).

The great 'if'

There is, then, an 'if' about the experience of the saving love of God: 'if you believe on Jesus'. There are alternatives involved: 'to have eternal life' or to 'perish'. Nothing is greater or mightier or more astonishing than God's love for sinners and His chosen way of salvation. But it is all focused on one point; miss that point and lose the blessing! For 'he who has the Son has life; he who does not have the Son of God does not have life' (1 John 5:12).

2

SPOTLIGHT ON IMMORTALITY

Even ordinary human experience ought to confirm for us the conclusion that God's love cannot be without conditions. There are few things on earth that we find more distasteful than the doting parental 'love' which produces the 'spoilt child'. In such circumstances we see that true love, whatever else it is, is moral in character and righteous in its outworking. It cannot be a loose, unvaried 'feather bedding' of all people at all times regardless of their character and conduct.

The next question to ask, however, is this: if the love of God is being offered to people here on earth, facing them with an 'either/or' decision to accept or reject Jesus Christ, is that love equally offered in the world to come? But if we were to proceed at once to this question we would find ourselves unprepared to answer it, for the answer depends on the existence and the nature of that world, and we must consider these matters first.

Revelation in Christ

The Lord Jesus Christ has 'destroyed death, and has brought life and immortality to light through the gospel' (2 Tim. 1:10). This is a wonderful truth, and wonderfully expressed here by Paul. In the Lord Jesus two things have come out into broad daylight – life and immortality. When we study Him, His life and teaching, His death and saving work, we see what life really is and how it may be obtained; we also see the life immortal as it really is, and how it may be obtained. The full spotlight of revelation shines on the life beyond the grave.

This does not mean that nothing was known about life after death before the Lord Jesus Christ came. Just as the Lord's people in the Old Testament enjoyed life in His fellowship, as the Psalms make so clear (e.g. 18:1, 2; 91:1, 2; 121:3-8), so also they had true perceptions about their expectations after death. In fact, the Bible evidences a clear progression from truth to more truth on this point, a cumulative revelation.

Life after death

The great assumption of the Old Testament is that life continues beyond the grave. It lies behind the beautiful description of Abraham who 'died at a good old age, an old man, and full of years, and he was gathered to his people' (Gen. 25:8). We might have expected something different to be said of the great man of faith – that he went to be with God, for example – but the description as it stands is a telling revelation of the reality which life after death possessed for those ancient times. He went to join the company of all his who had gone before; a truth which does not lose its attractiveness or its comfort with the passing of the years and the brightness of new revelation. Jacob too nourished the same hope in respect of his son

Joseph whom he presumed dead: 'I will go down to Sheol to my son mourning' (Gen. 37:35).

'Sheol'

Sheol in the Old Testament is a place-name and ought never – notwithstanding the NIV – to be represented as 'grave' or 'hell' or anything else. It is the name of the place to which the dead go, and all alike go there. Jacob assumed the good, if (at that time) rather priggish, Joseph to be there, and indicated the same destination for himself (Gen. 42:38). Likewise to Sheol went those who died under the wrathful judgment of God, when 'the earth opened its mouth, and swallowed them up ... and they ... went down alive into Sheol' (Num. 16:33). Sheol is the destination of the adulterer (Prov. 7:27), of those killed in war (Isa. 5:14), and of the heathen too (Isa. 14:9-15). It is the place of all the dead alike, good and bad, dying in their beds or in battle, belonging to the people of God or outside that privileged company.

What a testimony this is to the fact of life after death! All live on in Sheol. David expected to meet again the infant who died soon after birth (2 Sam. 12:23), and Job, in his misery, longed for the place where 'the wicked cease from turmoil, and ... the weary are at rest. Captives also enjoy their ease together ... the small and great are there; and the servant is freed from his master' (Job 3:17-19). While opinions differ on the interpretation of what the Old Testament tells about the *nature* of life in Sheol, there can be no disputing its insistence on the *fact* of life in Sheol. Life here on earth is not the complete span for humans; beyond it there is another and different existence which they cannot avoid, for 'what man can live and not see death, or save himself from the power of Sheol?' (Ps. 89:48).

Old Testament hope

In popular thought, Old Testament folk viewed their inevitable death and departure to Sheol much as some today speak of death as synonymous with the greatest trouble that could possibly happen, the most dreaded of all eventualities. 'The snares of death' are synonymous with the critical troubles of life (Ps. 18:5; 86:13; Jonah 2:2), in much the same manner as people still speak popularly of being 'frightened to death' or 'feeling deadly'. We do not intend to make a precise theological pronouncement about death when we speak like this; we are using the language of every day, the language natural and proper for those to use who find life on earth a good thing and a blessing from God.[1]

Paul, however, offers us a different and more biblical perspective when he contrasts heaven and earth as light and darkness, or maintains that to be 'with Christ' is 'far better' (Rom. 13:12; Phil. 1:23). Is there anything corresponding to this in the Old Testament? Did they have a *hope* (as distinct from mere continuance of life) beyond the grave?

Opinion on this point varies among Old Testament specialists, but present tendencies are not quite so firmly set as once they were against seeing a doctrine of hopeful

---

[1] Some verses in the Psalms are often interpreted as indicating that the Old Testament entertained no hope after death: 6:5; 30:9; 88:10ff.; 115:17. See also Isaiah 38:18. Note, however, (1) In all these verses except 115:17 the psalmist understands himself to be dying under divine displeasure. His words therefore do not refer to the state of the dead in general but to *his own lack of hopeful expectation at that moment*, as one dying without peace with God. (2) In Psalm 115 it should be noted that verse 18 envisages praise 'for evermore'. It would be wrong to interpret verse 17 as suggesting that praise stops at death. Behind the psalm lies a deadly crisis which would have silenced the earthly praise of the Lord (v. 17) but for divine intervention. On all these passages see J. A. Motyer, 'Psalms' in the *New Bible Commentary*, 21st Century Edition, IVP, 1994.

immortality in ancient Israel. One writer can maintain that 'the exegetical study which we propose to undertake here will enable us to show ... how the Old Testament ... proclaims, at first hesitantly and then with more assurance, the resurrection of the dead.'[2]

Psalm 49, 'In the morning'

Two Psalms must suffice for our consideration here, but see also, for example, Job 19:25; Psalm 16:8ff.; Psalm 17:14f.; Isaiah 26:19; 53:10ff.; Ezekiel 37:1-7; Daniel 12:2f.[3] In Psalms 49 and 73 the same problem is faced: the seeming injustice of life on earth, the way in which people of open ungodliness are often more prosperous than those devoted to God. How can the godless prosper and the righteous suffer?

In Psalm 49 the similarity of verses 12 and 20 indicates the two divisions of the subject. In the first twelve verses, the writer points out that death itself is no solution to life's inequalities, seeing that wise and foolish alike die: it is an inevitable human experience, because man for all his speciality dies like any other animal. But the second section of the Psalm brings us face to face with the situation beyond the grave, and it will help us to set out the key verses (14, 15) as follows:

(a) Like sheep they are destined for Sheol;
(b) Death will (lit.) shepherd them;
(c) And the upright will rule over them in the morning.

---

[2] R. Martin-Achard, *From Death to Life*, Oliver and Boyd, 1960, p. 51.

[3] See J. A. Motyer, *The Prophecy of Isaiah*, IVP, 1993; 'Psalms', as above; S. Ferguson, 'Daniel', *New Bible Commentary*, as above. Some English Translations of Psalm 49 (e.g. RSV, NRSV) emend the Hebrew text so as to make verses 12 and 20 identical. There is no warrant for this. NIV 'riches' is a particularly poor interpretative rendering. See KJV, RV, ESV for literal rendering.

(a) And their form shall be for Sheol to consume far from their princely mansions;

(b) But God will redeem my soul from the power of Sheol;

(c) For He will take me.

These verses speak of two distinct sets of people: the ungodly ('they'), and the godly ('me'). Seeing the six statements balanced against each other as indicated by the letters above, the two (a)-statements depict the wicked dwelling in Sheol, and entirely in Sheol's power. This is made explicit by the first (b)-statement: they have passed into death's governorship; but the other (b)-statement indicates a different governorship for the righteous, an act of God redeeming the soul from Sheol. Finally the two (c)-statements exhibit a destiny of the righteous which contrasts emphatically with that which the (a)-lines portrayed for the wicked: whatever be their respective positions on earth, with the righteous often being the underdogs, after death a different pattern is evident, for the righteous have dominion 'in the morning' – that is, in the time of hope – and God receives them to Himself.

Psalm 73, 'Afterwards'[4]

Psalm 73:23f. provides another statement of the same hope. The Psalmist, facing the same problem of life as that in Psalm 49, counts his blessings and notes his present fellowship with God: 'I am always with you'; he next reckons on his present security, for 'you hold me by my right hand'; then he looks forward into the future with confidence, because 'you guide me with your counsel'; and, finally, he dares to look beyond death and is undismayed,

---

[4] A. M. Fairhurst, 'Death and Destiny', *Churchman*, 95/4/1981, pp. 313-325. The notes to this important article provide a useful bibliography.

knowing that 'afterwards you will take me into glory.' It is important to note that the same verb 'to take' expresses the heavenly welcome here as well as in Psalm 49:15. Its use also in Genesis 5:24 and 2 Kings 2:9 makes it something of a technical term in the Old Testament vocabulary of eternal hope. The clear progression from present to future and then to 'afterwards' in Psalm 73:23, 24 is eloquent testimony to a sure hope beyond the grave.[5]

Moral distinctions

The implication is clear in Psalm 49:14, 15, as set out above, that Sheol is a place where moral and spiritual distinctions are preserved. There is a blessedness for the people of God, and there is an adversity for those who rejected or denied Him on earth. So that for all his speciality as a human being compared with the merely animal creation, if a person dies without understanding (Ps. 49:20), without having come to personal knowledge of God and fellowship with Him, it is a denial of all that humankind was distinctively created for and is to that extent comparable to the death of a beast.

The point made in verses 12 and 20 of Psalm 49 is not, of course, that a beast, at death, goes into adversity but that it is possible for humankind to die as beasts do. In the case of humans, such thoughtless death carries with it the loss of eternal felicity.

On this aspect of death – the prospect of an adverse immortality – the Old Testament is, however, uniformly vague, with Daniel 12:2 as its most explicit statement of an eternal loss. Nevertheless, though still reticent on

---

[5] Contrast the translations offered in the NIV, ESV, NKJV and NRSV. Some translators are hesitant about any reference to '(heavenly) glory' in Ps. 73:24. The majority meaning, however, of the key word is: "glory", and, as indicated above, the sequence of thought in the verse clearly suggests a reference to destiny after death.

detail, a passage such as Ezekiel 3:16-20 warns the wicked of the dreadful possibility of 'dying in sin'. This must be the intention of the watchman's warning. It is no warning to say that the wicked will die, and then leave it at that, for all die alike, and wickedness neither increases nor decreases the probability of death. Nor, on the basis of daily experience, does wickedness necessarily increase the likelihood of an earlier or more sudden death, as the NIV seems to imagine, for it often appears to be the good man who is cut off while the wicked lives to a great age!

What then was the content of Ezekiel's threat? Precisely the dreadful seriousness of entering the next world with sin unconfessed, unrepented and unforgiven!

Full light

When we step from the Old to the New Testament we come into the full light of all that God has chosen to tell us about the world to come. We have purposely given the greater part of our space in this chapter to the Old Testament, for its teaching is commonly ignored and often misunderstood, and it will suffice here simply to open up quite briefly what the New Testament teaches.

On one side there is a progression from hope to more glorious hope. The Psalmist was able to expect that God would receive him; Christians can say that they go to be with Christ which is far better (Phil. 1:23), that they will be 'for ever with the Lord' (1 Thess. 4:17), that the Lamb Himself will be their shepherd (Rev. 7:17), that they will see His face (Rev. 22:4), and that, in general, 'eye hath not seen, nor ear heard, neither have entered into the heart of man, the things which God hath prepared for them that love him' (1 Cor. 2:9). Thus immortality has been illuminated.

But what of the other side of the picture? We have said that the Old Testament hardly touches the topic of an adverse destiny of the wicked, but it is a striking fact that the New Testament, wherein the love of God is fully seen and where the blessed hope shines fully, seems to say the most terrible things about the lot of those who reject the gospel of our Lord Jesus Christ.

Jesus Himself was, indeed, the one to speak of 'eternal fire' and 'eternal punishment' (Matt. 25:41, 46); Paul recalled the words of the Lord in his reference to the 'flaming fire' by which vengeance would be taken on 'those who do not know God and do not obey the gospel', who would 'be punished with everlasting destruction and shut out from the presence of the Lord' (2 Thess. 1:8, 9); and John takes us into the very High Court of heaven itself where the judgment of 'the second death' (Rev. 20:13, 14) is passed.[6]

These words and ideas are extraordinarily terrible. The description of 'second death', a death which follows death, is striking and fearful. We must resolutely turn to the study of these things.

[6.] J. Blanchard, *Whatever happened to Hell?*, Evangelical Press, 1993.

3

WELCOME ALLEVIATION

Death is serious from every point of view. It marks the end of earthly contact with loved ones and, whatever lies beyond, it severs their contact with a world and a life which was not wholly undesirable but was maybe in most cases even extremely pleasant. If, however, we believe the Bible, none of these considerations comes anywhere near describing just why death is so serious. Three things are held together in the Bible, and there is no separating them: sin, death and judgment.

Sin and death
God's first word of command in Eden contained the warning of death: 'In the day you eat of it, you will surely die' (Gen. 2:17). We are not told what our condition would have been had the first couple abstained from the forbidden tree, but it seems reasonable to suppose that natural mortality would have been held in abeyance by a life of obedience to God and by access to the tree of life. Thus disobedience opened the floodgates to death, and that not the death an animal dies, the falling to the ground

of a carcase, but specifically, death because of sin against God, death under God's displeasure.

The wages of sin

For humankind, then, death is indeed 'the wages of sin' (Rom. 6:23).[1] It is a natural thing inasmuch as it takes place (as we say) in the course of nature, but much more is it a supernatural thing because it is an aspect of the relation of fallen, sinful beings to a holy and sin-hating God. Death, as Paul says, has a 'sting', a power to hurt, when a person dies in sin, because the inward accusations of sin spoken through the conscience are confirmed by the Word of God spoken in condemnation of sin and sinners in His law (1 Cor. 15:56). And how shall it go with those who enter the presence of God unforgiven?

According to the Bible, the lot of those who 'know not God, and ... obey not the gospel of our Lord Jesus' is to 'suffer punishment, even eternal destruction from the face of the Lord' (2 Thess. 1:8, 9). We must not be surprised that this should be so. In the Bible, sin is a fearfully serious thing, and a deadly destroyer. Even to us, some sins are so repugnant that we are prepared to acknowledge how right it is that those who commit them are put away out of the sight of their fellowmen. What must sin be like to a holy God?

None the less, the idea of eternal ruin or of eternal destruction from God's presence simply cannot be allowed to continue as a possibility if there is any permissible way of escaping from it. Every sensitive spirit will shrink from it and welcome any hope of alleviation.

Avenues of Alleviation

Two such avenues of alleviation now open before us. Neither is an attempt to minimize the seriousness of sin;

---

[1] Cf. S. W. Sykes, 'Death and Doctrine', *Churchman* 95/4/1981, pp. 306-312; S. Travis, *Christian Hope and the Future of Man*, IVP, 1981.

each is a way of escape from the horror involved in taking the New Testament threats of endless anguish in what appears at first sight to be their plain meaning.

(1) *Universalism*

The doctrine of universalism is unambiguous: everyone without exception has been chosen by God to enjoy eternal life through Christ, and God will personally see that each one comes into that enjoyment. It has been put like this in one of the most attractive statements of universalism ever to be written:

> In Adam *all* die, but in Christ *all* are made alive. That is the Divine 'nevertheless' beyond all hope, or merit. It rests on no condition of virtue or spirituality, but solely on the unconditional love of God. Consequently, *all* will be raised.[2]

And elsewhere like this:

> God is the Lord – therefore he wills that all should be interpreted by his Lordship ... God is love, therefore he wills to impart himself to all creatures. God is omnipotent, therefore there can be nothing ultimately to check the realization of his will.[3]

Scriptural support

The advocates of universalism argue that it rests on certain clear teachings of Scripture, in the light of which, as they would urge, other passages which present the stark eternal alternatives of life and death must be judged.

---

[2] J. A. T. Robinson, *In the End, God*, SCM 1958, p. 81; cf., F. W. Farrar, *Eternal Hope*, London 1878; J. P. Smyth, *The Gospel of the Hereafter*, London, 1964. Also the 'qualified universalism' as it seems of D. L. Edwards, *The Last Things Now*, SCM, 1969, pp. 71-78.

[3] E. Brunner, *Eternal Hope*, London 1954, p. 182.

Let us take, for example, as Brunner does, the parable of the sheep and the goats: it is a judgment scene; a clear separation is made of two classes by the Judge; and the alternatives of eternal punishment and eternal life are stated (Matt. 25:31-46). What could be clearer? Yet there are also verses which seem equally plain that all will be saved: 'As in Adam all die, even so in Christ shall all be made alive' (1 Cor. 15:22). Brunner's solution of this problem of interpretation is to see the message of the parable in the light of those verses which he believes favour universalism. The parable may suggest stark alternatives, but in fact it is 'the word of Jesus ... calling for decision ... exhorting to penitence and promising grace'. The point of the parable is to shatter self-assurance, and to leave salvation a possibility for all.[4]

But surely this is precisely what the parable is not! Certainly, everything that is true about our eternal destiny must exercise some pressure on us now, as Brunner suggests: to examine whether we have grounds for believing ourselves saved, to repent, to abandon self-confidence, and so forth. But if the parable is to be taken seriously at all – not necessarily as a blueprint of the Day of Judgment – it must set before us true principles concerning that Day. And three things seem clear: first, that on the Day of Judgment it will not be a matter of God's summoning people to repent, but of His declaring what their state before Him is, a day of pronouncing, not of inviting. Secondly, the parable indicates that the decision of that Court settles matters eternally. And thirdly, that judgment will be pronounced, there will be a division and not all will be saved.

---

[4] Brunner, as above, p. 180.

Defining God as 'love'

But what then about 'even so in Christ shall all be made alive'? Pausing briefly to mention that the passage here quoted seems itself to limit this 'all' to 'those who belong to Christ' (1 Cor. 15:23), and that some such limitation is present in every seemingly 'universal' passage, it is better to approach these claims along another line.

Universalists teach that because God's will is 'to sum up all things in Christ' (Eph. 1:10), all must be saved, else the will of God will have two results and not one, for if any should be lost, then in their case Omnipotent Love will have failed.

The issues raised here are enormous, and for the moment all we must do is ask one question and hope to attempt a fuller answer in the next chapter: Is 'love' a sufficient summary of the nature of God? The impeccable logic of Brunner, as quoted above, depends on answering this question in the affirmative. But suppose that there were other things to be said about God, equally true or even more true, might it not be that 'summing up all things in Christ' did not necessarily involve universal salvation? The 'logic of love' must, at the very least, be kept in touch with the 'logic of justice': the former says 'God is love, therefore all must be saved' but the latter – with equal biblical support – says 'God is just, therefore none can be saved'. To turn from Scripture to logic or to lose the balance and blending of scriptural doctrines in the interests of logic is a high road to error.

Human freedom

One other problem vexes the universalist position: what of human freedom? If all in the long run are to be saved, and in this life some freely reject the love of God, how can their freedom be respected if at the end they too become the objects of His loving salvation? And, if they have that love forced upon them, can they be said truly to respond to it?

Since there is no evidence in the Bible or outside it on which this question could be answered, the universalist appeals to a reasonable analogy. People may begin to 'fall in love' almost 'against their will', grudgingly won over by the attractiveness of someone else. Is their freedom violated? And 'may we not imagine a love so strong that ultimately no-one will be able to restrain himself from free and grateful surrender?'[5]

Two lines of reply can be indicated. Firstly, there is here an inevitable slur on the character of God, for if this is what will eventually happen, then all that He said – throughout the New Testament but especially through the Lord Jesus – about hell, with its fires and its punishments, is nothing less than an attempt to bluff people into loving Him. He becomes like the very worst sort of schoolteacher who, having failed to make His subject intrinsically attractive, and being without any personal charm to make up for this deficiency, resorts to threats which at last He lacks the strength of character to enforce.

The Cross

But, more important than this, what of Calvary? We have already noted that the love of God was demonstrated, proved and offered at the Cross. Can God ever give a greater proof? What do universalists mean when they speak of some overwhelming demonstration of God's love in the world to come? The centrepiece of that world is 'the Lamb as though it has been slain' (Rev. 5:6), that is, the Christ of Calvary. Why should people love Him then if they refuse Him now? And what greater proof or offer of love could God plan?

---

[5] Robinson, as above, p. 111.

(2) *Conditional immortality*

The second alleviating doctrine is described as conditional immortality. Since humans are not inherently immortal, but only become so by virtue of union with God, then according to this view, in default of faith and obedience, God will pronounce on such His sentence of annihilation. Dr John R. W. Stott, with customary exactness, draws attention to a distinction between 'annihilationism' and 'conditional immortality':

> According to the latter nobody survives death except those to whom God gives life ... whereas according to the former, everybody survives death and will even be resurrected, but the impenitent will finally be destroyed.[6]

Not all writers on this subject observe this distinction or even find it helpful and, in general, 'conditional immortality' is used (as we shall use it) as an 'umbrella' title. The two views, however, have one common point: either way, the problem of eternal punishment is alleviated – albeit at the expense of life itself. Both not infrequently share with universalism one common ground:

> I can hardly imagine two propositions more discordant one with the other, than that Almighty God is love, and that he will torment sinners for ever.[7]

This, as we have seen, depends for validity on the completeness of 'love' as descriptive of the divine nature.

---

[6] J. R. W. Stott and D. L. Edwards, *Essentials, A Liberal-Evangelical Dialogue,* Hodder and Stoughton, 1988, p. 316.

[7] T. Davis, *Endless Suffering Not a Doctrine of Scripture*, London 1867, p. 56. This is not true of the biblically thought-out positions of such as J. R. W. Stott and J. W. Wenham but it does disfigure much, specially universalist, thinking. See Note 8.

Defining 'Death'

A second ground of conditional immortality is its definition of death: 'All that God purposed to inflict upon Adam and his posterity in case of transgression is included in the word "death". It is of the utmost consequence then that we should understand what God meant by death ... its meaning, then, we contend to be, when it is thus attached to sin as its penalty, the loss of life or existence.'[8]

Thus, to die is to come to an end, unless an immortal life has been imparted through Christ.

But what, it may be asked, about the terms in which the adverse destiny of the unsaved is couched in the New Testament, and especially the word 'eternal'? The reply of conditional immortality is that this describes a result rather than a state. An eternal punishment is one which

---

[8] H. Constable, *The Duration and Nature of Future Punishment*, London 1886, p. 16. This work defends Conditional Immortality, as does H. E. Guillebaud, *The Righteous Judge*, Taunton, 1964; B. F. C. Atkinson, *Life and Immortality*, Taunton 1969. See also the biblically sensitive advocacy of annihilationism by J. W. Wenham, *The Case for Conditional Immortality*, Rutherford House, 1991 and, especially, J. R. W. Stott in *Essentials* (with D. L. Edwards, as above) pp. 312-320. The reaction of some that these biblical and evangelical men 'do not believe in Hell/in eternal judgment', that they 'have sold the pass' etc., is disappointingly superficial and takes scant note of what they actually say. We all alike wrestle with Scripture, seeking to do so with integrity, asking the question (Stott, p. 315), 'not what does my heart tell me, but what does God's Word say.' Our calling is to live and love as brethren within the bounds of the inspired Scripture, not to act and react as if our own poor interpretations were verbally inspired! In favour of Conditional Immortality see *The Fire That Consumes* by W. Fudge (Paternoster, 1994). This is a far-reaching inquiry into both biblical and extra-biblical sources and has produced a study that must be taken seriously. Nevertheless, though he writes at greater length it is hard to see that he has added in substance to the positions taken more succinctly by Stott and Wenham. See the very just review of Fudge by P. M. Head in *Anvil* Vol. 12, No. 3, 1995, pp. 271, 272. Against Conditional Immortality, see particularly J. Blanchard, *Whatever happened to Hell?* as above.

has eternal consequences, but need not itself be a conscious everlasting experience, and an eternal destruction is an act such as annihilation which can never be reversed.

We started this chapter by welcoming any relief from the terrors of 'eternal punishment'. We have now surveyed two such alleviating theories. The question remains: are they true?

4

THREE QUESTIONS

The last chapter left three important matters undecided. Both universalism and conditional immortality rested part of their case on certain conclusions drawn (with seemingly secure logic) from the truth that 'God is love'. Are these conclusions well founded? Is 'love' a sufficient description of God?

Conditional immortality, however, proceeded to two other supports: first, that death can be defined as 'the end' in an absolute sense, and, secondly, that the word 'eternal' must be understood as defining the nature of God's act of justice towards unrepentant sinners – indicating that it cannot ever be reversed – rather than as implying an endless consciousness on their part that they are the lost. Are these definitions correct? Do they bear biblical investigation?

Selective logic
When people speak of 'finding God in nature' it usually transpires that they are identifying God with a selection of the facts of the universe:

> The kiss of the sun for pardon,
> the song of the birds for mirth.
> One is nearer God's heart in a garden
> than anywhere else on earth.

But equally,

> The surge of the flood for pardon,
> the roar of the storm for mirth.
> One is nearer God's heart in an earthquake
> than anywhere else on earth.

God is in the beauty of sunset, the glory of the mountains, the freshness of the spring breeze, the order and wonder of the stars. But the natural world also contains storms of terrible ferocity, volcanoes with tragic consequences, floods, earthquakes and predatory beasts. Is not God in these also?

In exactly the same way, when people say 'God is love', they are selecting one out of many things that the Bible says about Him. Indeed, the very same portion of Scripture which contains these words also says that 'God is light' and that God 'is righteous' (1 John 1:5; 2:29; 4:8); it insists on His moral holiness and His inflexibly just activity. Have not these an equal claim to be heard?

(1) Love and wrath
It is not easy to come to a single definition of the divine nature. Alongside the incredibly benevolent God of Genesis 2, ever thoughtful for Adam's welfare (see especially Gen. 2:8, 18), there is the God of Genesis 3, with His stern questions, His imposition of a curse on that which He had earlier given in blessing (Gen. 3:16f.) – blighting marriage and nature, the two areas of special benevolence mentioned in 2:8, 18 – and His personal action in driving out the first pair and placing a flaming sword to prevent their

return (Gen. 3:24). For they left Eden, not by their own desire to escape God (Gen. 3:8), but by God's unwillingness to allow them to stay.

What Genesis thus establishes, the rest of the Bible confirms. Alongside the God who is 'a consuming fire, a jealous God', there is 'a merciful God', who 'will not abandon you, or destroy you, or forget the covenant' (Deut. 4:24, 31). In a word, the revelation of God in Scripture has many facets: severity (Isa. 5:25; Acts 5:1-11), power (Ps. 89:8; Eph. 1:19), wisdom (Dan. 2:20-23; Rom. 11:33) and majesty (Isa. 57:15; Rev. 5:13), to mention but a few, are all claimants along with love as constituents of the divine nature.

The same contrasts occur, however, in the Lord Jesus, yet all of them are unified into one Person. There is the whip of John 2:15 and the gentleness of Luke 8:54, the denunciations of Matthew 23:13ff. and the pardoning love of Luke 23:34, 43; there is power (Mark 4:39ff.), wisdom (John 7:46; Matt. 13:54), majesty (John 18:6) and much, much more, but only one perfect Lord Jesus Christ.[1] This is surely the significant point: the character of God, seen in the Lord Jesus, is a complete unity; there is no warring of attributes. We must never imagine that the existence of love and wrath in the same nature is evidence of a split personality, but only evidence that God is greater than can be grasped in our finite logic.

Holiness
The one divine attribute which more than any other is suggested by the Bible as a sufficient description of God is 'holiness'.

---

[1] P. Lewis, *The Glory of Christ*, Hodder and Stoughton, 1992; J. Blanchard, *Will the Real Jesus Please Stand Up?*, Evangelical Press, 1989; H. C. Hewlett, *The Glories of Our Lord*, Ritchie, 1994; N. T. Wright, *Who was Jesus?*, SPCK, 1992.

This attribute, implicit throughout Genesis, first became explicit at the Exodus where the whole sequence of events is bracketed about by the Lord's unapproachable and awesome holiness. At the start, Moses is warned that it is the Holy One who addresses and sends him (Exod. 3:5); and at the end, with the people gathered at Mount Sinai, Moses must make a special journey down the mountainside to add a further warning of the consequence of violating the holy presence of God (Exod. 19:20-25).

The same is true when the redeeming work of God, foreshadowed in the Exodus, is fulfilled at Calvary. The Cross of Christ is terrible, in the strict sense of the word. Here, to be sure, the love of God was given its supreme display and proof, yet it was here that the Saviour cried out, 'My God, my God, why have you forsaken me?' (Mark 15:34). If this means anything which we can grasp, it must mean this, that when Jesus 'became sin' for us (2 Cor. 5:21), the Holy God turned away from Him, unable and unwilling to tolerate such a one in His pure presence – just as of old He expelled the first sinners from Eden.

The Holy Name
Such a view is true to the biblical evidence. The threefold 'Holy' of Isaiah 6:3 is specially noteworthy. Hebrew uses repetition to express a superlative or to focus some quality as comprehensively true of its possessor. No quality, however, is raised elsewhere 'to the power of three' as Isaiah raises God's holiness.

The Lord is the super-superlatively Holy One, and holiness is the utterly comprehensive definition of His nature. But of equal significance, for example, is the fact that God's Name is described as His 'Holy Name' more often than all other descriptions taken together, for 'name' is shorthand for 'all that the Lord has revealed himself to be'.

If, therefore, we are to be true to our foundation documents, we cannot omit from our description of God the whole dimension of holiness, and it is most important for our present study that we should not. Indeed, it ought by now to be clear that any such simple scheme as that proposed by universalism is out of the question. There is more to God than love.

Furthermore, the highly emotional appeal that God cannot be imagined as condemning anyone to eternal torment must be reckoned as suspect. If we are frank, we would admit that we rarely see sin as a serious thing; our consciences will not even stretch to seeing why God was so 'intolerant' towards Adam and Eve (Gen. 3), or Uzziah (2 Chron. 26:16-21), or to Ananias and Sapphira (Acts 5:1ff.), or any others who came under His wrath. In other words, our fallen moral sense is no gauge to the reactions of a Holy God, and we need to beware of imprisoning the Almighty within the meagre grasp of our sinful nature (Isa. 55:8f.; 1 Cor. 1:19; 2:14).[2]

Moral distinctiveness
'God only knows the love of God,' wrote Charles Wesley, and it is true. In our experience, love is (to however small an extent) intermingled with self-centredness. What love is like when it resides in a pure Self, only God knows. But equally we must learn from Him what His holiness is, for on this subject maybe more than any other the Fall has necessarily left us purblind.

Two main ideas are contained in the biblical definition of holiness[3], and both are exemplified in Isaiah 6, the Bible's

---

[2] E. M. Goulburn, *Everlasting Punishment*, London, 1880, especially chapter 3. Goulburn 'observes' that 'it is not from Scripture that objections "to the doctrine of everlasting punishment" are really drawn, but from the reasonings and speculations of the human mind'. This is true of many, but not all, writers on this theme.

central section on this subject. Isaiah was first shown God in his remoteness, 'high and lifted up', *separate* from the world and people. Von Rad, in a memorable phrase, catches the feeling when he speaks of the Holy One as 'the great stranger in the human world'[4], yet even this is a negative idea, as if God's holiness simply made Him 'separate from' us. In the Bible, however, the separateness of holiness is positive: holiness expresses all that makes God His unique Self. Indeed, as Isaiah went on to learn, it is not so much a question of God being separate from us as that we are *separated* from God. For the second meaning urged for 'holy' is 'that which is splendid, bright, terrible', and in Isaiah's experience it is the moral character of God which contains this blazing terror for sinners.

Isaiah, the sinner, found himself to be banished from the presence of such a God, and was compelled to cry, in agony of spirit, 'Woe is me! For I am ruined!' (6:5). There is that in the nature of God which means ruination for sinners. Yet the actual sin which Isaiah confessed seems (to us) a comical anticlimax! 'I am a man of unclean lips,' said the prophet – but we hardly recognize this as *sin* at all! Certainly not such as brings ruination! Isaiah, however, experienced a moment of truth. He saw sin as it appears in the awesome splendour and terror of the divine holiness, and he saw also that holiness is not a passive state; it is the flashing forth of the pure moral glory and passion of God against anything and everything that offends Him. On this one side of its definition, God's holiness is His active intolerance of sin and so is often linked with the divine 'jealousy' as in Joshua 24:19f.

---

[3] J. B. Payne, *The Theology of the Older Testament*, Zondervan, 1962, pp. 123ff.; G. von Rad, *Old Testament Theology*, SCM 1962, pp. 204ff.; Th. C. Vriezen, *An Outline of Old Testament Theology*, Blackwell, 1960, pp. 149ff.; J. A. Motyer, *A Scenic Route Through the Old Testament*, IVP, 1995, p. 135.; *Look to the Rock*, IVP, 1996, p. 207.

[4] Von Rad, as above, p. 205.

It is no wonder, then, that we find it hard to come to terms with some of the biblical witness to the holiness of God: the fencing of Mount Sinai lest the people trespass on holy ground and 'the LORD break out against them' (Exod. 19:22), the smiting of the men of Beth-shemesh (1 Sam. 6:19), and of Uzzah (2 Sam. 6:6). Yet, as the epistle to the Hebrews emphasizes, God has not changed: He is still 'a consuming fire' (12:29); it is 'a dreadful thing to fall into the hands of the living God' (10:31). To a large extent our personal experience and our public religion are shallow and unimpressive for this very reason, that we have never feared the holiness of God, nor learned what it means to 'rejoice with trembling' (Ps. 2:11).

But, whatever our personal experience, it is a plain matter of honesty in handling Holy Scripture that we restrain ourselves from imposing our own logical constructions upon God. Someone, for example, asks: 'How, in the end, can "God be all in all" (1 Cor. 15:28) if there are souls in eternal torment?'; or, another may ask: 'How can "God be all in all" if he has "contrived" his supremacy by using omnipotence to annihilate the disobedient?' These questions can be continued endlessly: we can equally ask 'If God is love, how can anyone be lost?' and 'If God is holy, how can anyone be saved?' But all such reasoning can only mislead, for His ways are not our ways, nor are our thoughts His thoughts. We are in no position to say what conditions satisfy the divine supremacy. Holiness eludes us. We can only seek humbly to follow what is written for our learning.

(2) Is death the end?
We are thus unable to say that eternal punishment is out of the question on the grounds of the nature of God. Indeed, wording the issue more broadly, John Baillie remarks that

'it is doubtful whether the final supremacy of the Good
would be less compromised by the power of evil finally to
destroy souls that had been created in the divine image,
than it would be by the perdurance to all eternity of souls
in which sin remained for ever active but for ever under
punishment'.[5]

As we turn, then, to the second of the questions posed at
the beginning of this chapter, we find ourselves faced with
a consideration which is urged as determining the whole
issue. Conditional immortality defines death as the end
of existence and so there can be no question of lingering
eternally in pain because the 'wages of sin is death' and
death means the termination of life.

Is this so? If it were, of course, then our discussion is at
an end, but the Bible would not appear to see the matter
in this way.

'You shall surely die'

Adam was threatened with death if he disobeyed God
(Gen. 2:17) and, in fact, when he disobeyed, he became,
for the first time, subject to physical death, for had he
remained in Eden and chosen rather the Tree of Life, he
would have lived for ever (Gen. 3:22). But, as the story
indicates, sin brought the stamp of death into every area
of human life and relationships, and, in Paul's phrase,
'death reigned from Adam' (Rom. 5:14). He lost true life,
and he entered into a 'death-life'.

Adam died and yet he lived on, and it is in these terms
that Genesis 3 defines the idea of death. Death means a
change of state (from the fellowship and blessing of God
to alienation and God's curse), and a change of place (from
Eden to banishment), but with continuity of person and

---

[5] J. Baillie, *And the Life Everlasting*, OUP, 1961, pp. 188f.

character. This understanding of the story is rescued from the realm of fancy and established as a serious attempt to understand the nexus between sin and death by the observation that this is precisely what the rest of the Bible means by death: when people die they change from a body-soul state; they leave earth for Sheol, a change of place; but the person continues (Gen. 37:35; 1 Sam. 28:11ff.; 2 Sam. 12:23).[6]

'The second death'
Indeed, the discussion of the meaning of death, far from helping the cause of conditional immortality, points entirely to the traditional doctrine of eternal punishment. For there are no biblical grounds for saying that 'death means the end'. The unbroken witness of the Bible is that the dead are alive and that death ushers a person into a new sphere of life.

Since this is so, then, when the last judgment is followed by 'the second death', we have no liberty to assume that death has a meaning here other than that which it has borne throughout Scripture (Rev. 20:6, 14; 21:8). Following the giving of judgment, the 'second death' brings a change of state, those awaiting divine judgment have now received sentence; a change of place, Sheol being exchanged for the 'lake of fire'; but continuity of person and character.

Standing before God
One cannot write or contemplate these things without asking pardon for inadequacy of language, for our temporal, spatial terminology cannot be suited to accurate assessment of these eternal things. More than this, the heart cries out to be a universalist. But the facts, insofar as they are revealed or inferred, will not allow it.

---

[6] L. Morris, *The Wages of Sin*, IVP, 1955.

One thing is certain: death works no moral transformation. When the dead 'small and great' stand before God, 'the books are opened' (Rev. 20:12), which, pictorially, teaches that, no matter what 'length of time' has intervened between death and judgment, men and women appear before God in the robe of the character woven here on earth.

Those who hated God here will hate Him there; the morally careless in earthly life will be morally careless still; the defiant will continue defiant, and the unclean will remain uncleansed and unrepentant.

The rich man in Hades 'where he was in torment' (Luke 16:23), while he exhibited a concern that his brethren should not follow him there, was exactly the same person as before, still ready to subject Lazarus to his own whims, still concerned for bodily satisfaction, without expressed concern for God, desire for repentance, or awareness of spiritual loss. Death is not the end, either of life itself or of the varied expressions of life in individual character.

Eternal destruction

But, in this case, what are we to make of such an expression as 'eternal destruction', describing the condition of those who do not obey the gospel (2 Thess. 1:8ff)?[7] If words mean anything, surely this means that such people will be destroyed, that is to say, will be utterly brought to an end of existence, and that this is 'eternal' in the sense of 'never to be reversed'.

There is evidence in the New Testament to support this contention. The verb 'to destroy' (*apollumi*) is part of the relevant vocabulary, entering the discussion through our

---

[7] The word is *olethros*. None of the occasions on which it is used illuminate any specific meaning. 2 Thessalonians 1:9 specifies the fact of divine judgment; 1 Thessalonians 5:3, its suddenness; 1 Timothy 6:9, its cause. 1 Corinthians 5:5 is a verse whose meaning is unclear.

Lord's reference to the One whom in context He speaks of as 'the Father' and who is able to 'destroy both soul and body in hell' (Matt. 10:28). In other places it is used to describe total cessation of life or being, as when, for example, the Lord says it is better that one bodily member should 'perish' than that the whole body should be cast into hell (Matt. 5:29f.).

In the same way, the corresponding noun, 'destruction' (*apoleia*), is used in the severest possible meaning when Peter wishes that Simon's money may 'perish' (Acts 8:20). Likewise, considering the adjective 'eternal', there are examples of its use to describe an eternal result, as distinct from an eternal experience. Thus, 'eternal judgment' (Heb. 6:2)[8] points to a decision with eternal consequences, and 'eternal sin' (Mark 3:29) is one which can never be forgiven rather than one which is constantly being repeated.

If we take our lead from these examples, then the case for conditional immortality is well on its way to being established. But examination of the words mentioned shows that this is not their only shade of meaning, nor even, on the whole, their most typical. We must survey the ground again.

The verb 'to destroy' is used at least twenty-two times in the sense of 'to die' or 'to be killed'[9] but in these instances

---

[8] Wherever the adjective *aionios* is used the idea of 'endless duration' is present. This tells against universalism. D. L. Edwards, *The Last Things Now*, as above, page 62, says that 'in Classical Greek (e.g. Plato) the word meant "eternal" or "timeless"…'. Though Liddell and Scott (*A Greek-English Lexicon*, 8th Edition, OUP, 1897) do not register the meaning 'timeless' (*aionios*, 'lasting for an *aeon*, an age, dispensation, etc.), Edwards's suggestion is a helpful reminder that our present notions and experiences of time as duration do not apply to God or 'eternity'.

[9] Matthew 2:13; 8:25; 12:14; 21:41; 22:7; 26:25; 27:20; Mark 3:6; 4:38; 9:22; 11:18; 12:9; Luke 8:24; 11:51; 13:33; 15:17; 17:27, 29; 19:47; 20:16; 21:18; John 6:27; 11:50; Acts 5:37.

it carries no implication about the ensuing state: this must be decided in terms of the meaning of 'death'. It is used very often as an opposite to the idea of being 'saved'[10] but, again, without specifying the precise condition of the 'lost'.

Rather more precisely, it is used of those who die without hope (1 Cor. 15:18) or under the active judgment of God (Luke 13:3, 5; Rom. 2:12; 2 Pet. 3:6, 9; Jude 11), but again without being specific as to the state of these dead. Indeed, it can be used in as 'weak' a sense as 'to be spoiled' or diverted from proper function (Mark 2:22; John 10:10; Rom. 14:15; 1 Cor. 8:11).

Which of these senses does it have in those contexts which speak of the eternal state of the 'lost'? That they are annihilated? That they are under divine displeasure? That they have been warped away from the original design and are spoiled? Or simply that they are dead?

We need some fixed point of interpretation if we are to thread our way accurately here, but this at least must be clear, that the words cannot demand absolute cessation of conscious life. Those who 'perished with Korah' (Jude 11) 'went down alive into Sheol' (Num. 16:33) – dying under the direct judgment of God but not ceasing to exist.

The noun 'destruction' (also translated 'damnation', 'perdition' and 'waste') is equally indecisive. In the main, it is broadly descriptive of the wicked, as in the expression 'son of perdition' (John 17:12; 2 Thess. 2:3; cf. Rom. 9:22), or of their life, conduct and end (Matt. 7:13; Phil. 3:19; 2 Pet. 2:1, 2; 3:16; Heb. 10:39; cf. Phil. 1:28), or of the judgment of God upon them (2 Pet. 2:1; 3:7).

But in none of these references is there justification for drawing the conclusion that the word is equivalent to

---

[10] Matthew 18:14; Luke 6:9; 9:56; John 3:15f.; 10:28; 1 Corinthians 1:18; 2 Corinthians 2:15; 2 Thessalonians 2:10; James 4:12; Jude 5.

annihilation. Indeed, it is particularly important to observe that, in the book of Revelation, 'the beast' is described as destined 'to go to destruction/perdition', but this fate is more fully defined as 'the lake of fire ... where are also the beast and the false prophet; and they shall be tormented day and night for ever and ever' (17:8, 11; 19:20; 20:10). In addition to this grim significance, the same noun is used in the sense of 'waste' – 'To what purpose is this waste?' (Matt. 26:8) – with reference to the ointment poured on the Saviour but, in the estimation of the disciples, diverted from its proper and most profitable use.

(3) The word 'eternal'

The third question posed at the outset of this chapter touched on the significance of the word 'eternal', and we may start our brief review of it by recalling that it can refer to the endless result of an action – in this case, specifically, the act of God in judgment – but without necessarily involving an endless conscious experience of that result. It is here that the advocates of conditional immortality urge that we are not obliged by Scripture to suppose that those who come under divine judgment are eternally conscious of their lost state. They are, in fact, annihilated, brought to an end of all existence.

The question, therefore, that lies before us is this: while agreeing that God could, if He chose, annihilate souls in this way, and that this act would be eternal and irreversible in its effect, is the word 'eternal' so used in Scripture of the lot of the lost, or does Scripture suggest an eternal consciousness of their lost condition?

Vocabulary

There are three expressions central to the discussion: 'eternal destruction' (2 Thess. 1:9), 'eternal punishment' (Matt. 25:46), and 'eternal fire' (Matt. 25:41).

Taking these in order, it was pointed out earlier that the word here translated 'destruction' (*olethros*, see footnote 7) cannot be treated as self-interpreting. It points only to the judgment of God upon the wicked, and its meaning must be determined in the light of the total teaching of the Bible on this subject. It is significant, however, that in one place it is used alongside the noun 'destruction' (*apoleia*) discussed above: 'harmful desires that plunge men into ruin (*olethros*) and destruction (*apoleia*)' (1 Tim. 6:9). It must be noted, therefore, that the only place which defined the nature of 'destruction' (*apoleia*) did so in terms of the conscious experience of the 'lake of fire'. If this partnership of words suggests anything, it favours the doctrine of everlasting consciousness of loss.

'Eternal punishment'

The phrase 'eternal punishment' is used by our Lord Himself to describe the destiny of 'those on the left hand' who are condemned at the great Assize (Matt. 25:46). In classical Greek this word (*kolasis*) refers to punishment as applied to the offender – in contrast to *timoria* (Heb. 10:29) which is punishment satisfactory to the offended party or to the offence committed. Classical authors did use *kolasis* (and its related verb *kolazein*) in contexts suggesting 'correction' or the reformation of the offender – therefore referring to punishment directed to a remedial purpose and only lasting till that purpose was achieved – but, says Trench, 'it would be a very serious error ... to transfer this distinction in its entireness to the New Testament'.[11] The only other New Testament occurrence

---

[11] R. C. Trench, *Synonyms of the New Testament*, London 1894, pp. 24ff.; Liddell and Scott, *Lexicon,* as above, p. 43; C. Brown (Ed.) *Dictionary of New Testament Theology*, Paternoster 1975–1978, Vol. 1, p. 568, 'punishment as the reaction and answer to evil deeds, not as a means of education'; Vol. 3, pp. 98-100 (with bibliography).

of the noun (1 John 4:18) tells us nothing of the nature of the 'punishment' in mind. Acts 4:21 uses the verb of a (hopefully) reformative discipline, but there is no thought of reformation, only of punishment, in 2 Peter 2:9 and the same is true of the use of the noun in the Apocrypha (Wisdom 19:4; 2 Maccabees 4:38).

In Matthew 25:46, however, 'eternal punishment' can have only one meaning. The unbroken usage of the adjective 'eternal' includes the idea of 'endlessness' (however inadequate our vocabulary is at this point) and forbids us to go the way of universalism in saying that our Lord is teaching here a very long period of corrective detention. The notion of 'eternity' in the New Testament excludes the idea of termination; and the noun 'punishment' wherever it is used signifies painful experience. Furthermore, in Matthew this *kolasis* (punishment) is a sharing of the fate of 'the devil and his angels' (25:41), that is, the 'second death' (Rev. 20:10, 14) with all its frightful realities of a final and irreversible change of place and state along with continuing personal life. Indeed, can the precise terms used by our Saviour in this passage point in any other direction? Leon Morris observes that 'the same adjective is applied to both the punishment and the reward' – one group to 'eternal punishment' and 'the righteous' (v. 37) to 'eternal life':

> Jesus is not speaking of some small experience that would be but for a moment, but of that which has no end. He leaves his hearers in no doubt as to the solemnity of what he is saying. Eternal issues are involved, and this is so for both those on his right hand and on his left.[12]

---

[12] L. Morris, *The Gospel According to Matthew*, IVP, 1992, p. 641. The full note here and its related footnotes are deeply important.

'Eternal fire'

Our Lord was also responsible for the expression 'eternal fire' (Matt. 18:8; 25:41; Mark 9:43, 48; cf. Matt. 13:40, 42). Comparing Scripture with Scripture, it is clear that 'eternal' must here have the significance of 'ever-burning' rather than merely 'eternal in effect'. The passages in question are Matthew 18:8 and Mark 9:48. The former speaks of 'eternal fire', and the latter, recapitulating the same teaching of the Lord, quotes Him as saying that 'the fire is not quenched'. In both passages, as in the place at present being discussed, the topic is the destiny of the unsaved and we are therefore bound to hold that the intention of the divine Teacher is the same and His wording consistent.

But did He also teach that the unsaved would experience eternally this 'eternal fire'? Presumably an 'eternal fire' could burn on but yet annihilate once and for all those who are thrown into it. The rest of the New Testament is against this conclusion. Wherever it uses the Lord's imagery of the 'eternal fire', it seems to concur with His word that 'their worm does not die' (Mark 9:48). At the very least, it can be put this way, and as far as we can tell, the words would only have been understood in this one way by our Lord's hearers so that, had He not intended this meaning, He must either have avoided or else otherwise explained them. The origin of the expression is Isaiah 66:24, where the undying worm and the unquenched fire is the lot of 'the men that have transgressed against me'. The pathway whereby this reached the New Testament and the meaning it had for New Testament times may be discerned in references contained in the Apocrypha. Judith 16:17, with the same topic in hand, reads: 'The Lord Almighty will take vengeance of them in the day of judgment, to put fire and worm in their flesh, and they shall weep and feel their pain for ever'.[13]

---

[13] Ecclesiasticus 7:17. Full discussion in E. B. Pusey, *What is of Faith as to Everlasting Punishment?* London 1880, pp. 50ff. On Isaiah 66:23, 24, see Motyer, *Isaiah*, as above. See also J. I. Packer's sketch, *The Problem of Eternal Punishment*, Orthos, 1990, but noting Wenham's fair strictures.

It is a remarkable providence that the sternest teaching on the eternal state of the lost comes from the lips of Jesus.

> Christ on himself, considerate Master, took
> The utterance of that doctrine's fearful sound:
> The Fount of Love his servants sends to tell
> Love's deeds; himself reveals the sinner's Hell.[14]

No human voice or pen has sufficient love, sympathy, or sensitivity to raise these questions without giving more offence than even the doctrines themselves. But it was He, the Lord of love, who contrasted the two destinies: eternal punishment and eternal life. The very form of the contrast impels us to understand each in the same way, or else to charge the Teacher with intent to deceive. Eternal life, like eternal salvation (Heb. 5:9), eternal redemption (Heb. 9:12), and eternal inheritance (Heb. 9:15), presupposes eternal consequences which believers consciously enjoy. Eternal punishment, by parity of reasoning and teaching, must carry the same significance: a conscious experience of endless duration.

Appendix: **The Nature of Punishment**
So much offence is naturally caused by a literalistic approach to the 'fires' of punishment, that a note may be in place here on the nature and methods of divine judgment as the Bible reveals them.

(1) Judgment comes upon sin both by the direct action of God and by the outworking of the moral laws of divine providence which govern our life on earth. Sin both invites punishment and brings punishment. By its very nature it both provokes God and destroys the sinner. For example, in two successive pictures, Isaiah displays the double-sided punishment of Jerusalem in his day: 'this sin' is like a crack

---

[14] Pusey, as above, p.47.

bulging out in a wall – that is, its own internal pressures destroy the fabric; but also 'he shall break it as a potter's vessel is broken', that is, there is a direct, divine, punitive action (Isa. 30:13f.)[15] Providentially, sin is a calamitous process bringing its own inherent disaster (cf. Jas. 1:15); but also, judgmentally, there is a direct, personal activity of God. The same double activity, external and internal, is found when Jeremiah says: 'I will bring evil upon this people, the fruit of their thoughts' (Jer. 6:19). God brings the punishment, and sin brings the punishment. Thus, the punishment of the sinner is not an arbitrary vengeance but the due process of moral providence.

(2) Punishment therefore often comes about by God, as it were, leaving people to their own devices. Essentially sinners are self-sufficient. They do not realize that they can go on in seeming self-sufficiency only because the common grace of God, His universal, creatorial goodness (Ps. 104:24-30; Matt. 5:45; Acts 14:17), allows them to enjoy so many of life's satisfactions. But should God withhold this secret grace, what then? Isaiah supplies the picture: 'The bed is too short to stretch out on, and the blanket too narrow to wrap around you' (Isa. 28:20). What a picture of frustration and discomfort: the would-be sleeper stretches out and finds the bed too short, curls up and the blanket is no longer wide enough! Even so, humans left to themselves, far from being able to save themselves, cannot even satisfy themselves. They are altogether insufficient for their own needs. Romans 1:24, 26, 28 exposes the consequence of people being thus 'left' by God. This is one aspect of the outworking of His wrath, its this-worldly consequences; Ephesians 5:6 leans more towards the eternal judgment which the Holy God will yet impose.

---

[15] As KJV, RV. This is preferable to the impersonal rendering in NIV. See Motyer, *Isaiah*, as above.

(3) Fire is used in the Bible to symbolize both the holiness of God and the unsatisfied desire of man. In Ezekiel it is the fire of God's holiness that destroys the doomed city (Ezek. 10:2); Paul speaks of the 'burning' of unfulfilled desire (1 Cor. 7:9). When the Bible, therefore, speaks of eternal loss as 'fire' it is pictorializing a double reality: a conscious realization both of alienation from God and of burning, personal desires eternally deprived of satisfaction (cf. Luke 16:24).

5

CAN WE HELP?

The doctrine of eternal separation from God has often been handled by Christians in a hard and unfeeling manner, and indeed, no matter with what restraint and sensitivity one tries to speak of such things, the accusation of callousness is bound to be levelled. But must we not follow Scripture where it leads? However faultily a matter is expressed, the question is not one of literary style but of truth. Are we to place unrestricted reliance on our own powers of reasoning, as some universalists do, saying that because God is love all must be well for all alike, or are we to submit to Scripture?

Let this at least be said: to each is given by God the liberty to study the Bible individually and personally, and to decide what it means; many who have done this, while rejecting universalism, have concluded that the use of the word 'destruction' favours theories of annihilation or conditional immortality. Each must be personally persuaded, submissively to Holy Scripture.

The decisive present

There is one thing, however, which is completely agreed between those who hold to conditional immortality and those who hold the doctrine of everlasting punishment: *the decisive importance of this present life.*

God in Christ

The greatest reason for believing this to be so is that it was here, in this world, that God became incarnate in Christ, here that 'God was in Christ reconciling the world to himself' (2 Cor. 5:19) and commending 'his love in that while we were yet sinners Christ died for us' (Rom. 5:8). If the supreme decision can be made beyond the grave, and if (as universalists hold) the greatest display of divine love, which will finally sweep away all human unresponsiveness, waits to be made in heaven, why did God send His Son to be born *here* and to die *here*?

Our Lord, in a relevant case, lent His authority to the dictum that 'if they do not listen to Moses and the Prophets, they will not be convinced even if someone rises from the dead' (Luke 16:31): that is, if people do not submit to the revelation God has given them now, in this life, no supernatural display will convince them.

Consequently, and with reverence, may it be said, if they do not believe in and love God manifested in Christ crucified, there is nothing more that God will do, and there is nothing left to convince them. When God chose the stage of history for the enacting of the drama of redemption, He sealed for ever the decisiveness of this present life and the eternal consequences of the decisions made here about Christ.

No 'second chance'

This is no mere theorising from the fact of the incarnation, as though to say that logic requires this deduction to be made. In three successive verses John implies the impossibility of a 'second chance' after death (John 3:17-19). First, there is the fact and purpose of the coming of Christ: 'Not to judge the world; but that the world should be saved through him' (v. 17). In the biblical idiom of contrast, we have here a statement of God's *priority* in sending His Son into the world. He was moved by a purpose of salvation. The incarnation, aimed as it was at the atoning death of Christ – so that of Him alone it may and must be said that He was born in order that He might die – was motivated by grace and mercy and pity for sinners.

Secondly, this divine movement presents people with the alternatives of salvation or judgment here and now (v. 18). A person who believes in the Son of God passes out of the sphere of judgment and has a new relation to God, and it is no longer the relation of sinner to Judge. By contrast, however, 'whoever does not believe stands condemned already'. Consider the force of that adverb: *already*. To refuse Jesus Christ is to establish oneself in the 'sinner-Judge' relationship with God, as though the eternal verdict itself had already been passed. This is the decisiveness of the present life.

In the third place, John goes on to explain why this is so (v. 19). To refuse Christ is to side with 'darkness' against 'light', and to give one's loyalty to that which God hates and which hates God. It is, already now, to adhere to and confirm a relationship with all that 'darkness' implies, which can end only in destruction.

Purgatory

It is natural, however, to ask how we stand in relation to those loved ones who have 'departed this life'. Since we still love them can we not serve them in love as once we delighted to do when they were with us?

The answer of one section of Christendom is given in the doctrine of Purgatory. 'Purgatory' says the Catechism of the Catholic Church[1] is 'the final purification', for though 'all who die in God's grace and friendship, but still imperfectly purified, are indeed assured of their eternal salvation' yet 'after death they undergo purification so as to achieve the holiness necessary to enter the joy of heaven'. This includes an element of punishment for sin but 'something entirely different from the punishment of the damned.' Purgatory is 'a cleansing fire'.

Purgatory, then, is a specifically *Christian* institution. It is not a means whereby pagans can be brought to God; its sole function is to deal with the sinful state of Christians at death and to prepare them for the full reality of heaven.

Now, as regards this sinful state, there are two aspects of it: guilt and punishment. Guilt is forgiven, according to this view, through the priestly absolution of the Church, but punishment awaits the Christian after death. When Christians die, says Mohler, they 'are with reason included in the suffering Church; for their peculiar existence must be considered as one, not only still passing through the fire of purification, but as also subjected to punishment'.[2]

'The Treasury'
According to Roman Catholic teaching, souls in Purgatory may be granted some remission of sentence by the accrediting to them of the 'supererogatory' works of the

---

[1] *Catechism of the Catholic Church*, Geoffrey Chapmen, 1995, sections 1030-1032, p. 235.

[2] J. A. Mohler, *Symbolism, or Exposition of the Doctrinal Differences between Catholics and Protestants,* London, 1843, p. 343; G. Salmon, *The Infallibility of the Church*, London, 1923, chapter 13; W. E. Addis etc., *A Catholic Dictionary*, London 1960, 'Purgatory'; See also, and especially N.T. Wright, *For All the Saints: Remembering the Christian Departed*. SPCK, 2003.

saints, especially of the Virgin Mary and of our Lord who, in their lives, more than pleased God, and the overplus of their merits constitutes a treasury at the disposal of the Church.

Living Christians can accumulate such 'indulgence' or remission by the performance of specified 'good works', such as, for example, visiting the seven chief churches and privileged altars at Rome'.[3] Equally it is possible for indulgence to be granted to the faithful departed in Purgatory through the prayer of the Church on earth.

Chief among the means of gaining such remissions is the 'sacrifice of the Mass', the Council of Trent itself ruling that 'souls detained there are helped by the suffrages of the faithful ... specially by the acceptable sacrifice of the altar', but 'the Church also commends almsgiving, indulgences and works of penance undertaken on behalf of the dead.'[4]

The Reformation Settlement
Very large issues are raised here, and we must try to face them, not least because both the practice of 'the requiem celebration of the Holy Communion'[5] and the doctrine of Purgatory have reappeared in the Church of England.

---

[3] Addis, as above, 'Indulgences'; *Catechism of the Catholic Church*, as above, sections 1471-1479, especially 1477-1479.

[4] J. Waterworth, *The Canons and Decrees of the Council of Trent*, London, 1848, p. 232; *Catechism*, as above, section 1032.

[5] The-then Archbishop of Canterbury (A. M. Ramsay) held a 'requiem celebration of Holy Communion' in the chapel of Lambeth Palace at the death of Pope John XXIII in 1963. Within the Anglican Communion there are organisations such as 'The Guild of All Souls', existing 'to promote the Church's teaching in regard to the Faithful Departed, to pray for the dead ... to encourage Christian customs of burial ... to urge the Celebration of the Holy Sacrifice of the Mass at the time of burial... (and to provide) proper Vestments for Requiem Masses' (the official leaflet of the Guild).

The word 'reappeared' is here used advisedly, for the sixteenth-century Reformers leave us in no doubt what teaching they intended to bequeath to their church: 'The Romish doctrine concerning Purgatory, Pardons ... is a fond thing vainly invented, and grounded upon no warranty of Scripture'; 'The sacrifices of Masses, in which it was commonly said, that the Priest did offer Christ for the quick and the dead, to have remission of pain or guilt, were blasphemous fables, and dangerous deceits'.[6] We cannot dismiss this testimony simply on the ground that this is the twentieth and not the sixteenth century. The point at issue is one of truth, not of date. Were the Reformers right or wrong in their assessment?

The opinion of the cautious E. J. Bicknell[7] is that we must find room for a doctrine of Purgatory, firstly on grounds of antiquity, since 'such a belief has been widely held in various forms in all parts of the Church since the second century'; and secondly on grounds of rationality for 'when we consider the moral imperfection of so many who die in the faith of Christ and the impossibility of seeing God "without sanctification" (Heb. 12:14), it is almost impossible not to think that the life beyond the grave includes discipline through which the character is purified. Some form of Purgatory is almost an intellectual necessity.'

In the long run, as we shall see, all forms of purgatorial doctrine, however crude, however refined, come under the same condemnation that they deeply misunderstand the significance of the death of Christ, but we will pause briefly to consider some other issues raised by Bicknell's position.

---

[6] Articles 22 and 31 of the Thirty-Nine Articles of Religion, *The Book of Common Prayer.*

[7] E. J. Bicknell, *A Theological Introduction to the Thirty-Nine Articles,* Longmans 1944, pp. 248ff.

Reason and Scripture

In the first place, we must assert again the inadequacy of a merely logical argument. Intellectual pride is the last citadel to be surrendered to the grace of God, and it is nothing but unwarranted pride of intellect to say because we think it so then it must be so! The sin of the Sadducees lives on (Mark 12:14-27)!

Bicknell had earlier correctly emphasized the reticence of Christ and of Scripture about life after death. A like reticence in receiving the dictates of human logic would not have been misplaced. The antiquity of the opinion concerning Purgatory does nothing more than illustrate that from the immediately post-apostolic days the Church has been marred by non-biblical thinking. No amount of appeal to antiquity can contradict Bicknell's own admission that he is here departing from Scripture. He owns that 'the language of Scripture bids us view the state of the faithful departed as primarily one of rest and refreshment' but continues by appealing to the 'intellectual necessity' of a doctrine of Purgatory because of the moral imperfection of those who have died in Christ.

It may be, however, that Bicknell is guilty here of nothing more than a misuse of terms and a confusion of thought. Is he not confusing the *possibility* of moral *growth* after death with the *necessity* of purgatorial *discipline* after death? He speaks in the same passage of 'the purifying power of joy and thankfulness' as part of the believer's portion. The possibility of the growth of moral and spiritual character in the world to come is certainly not to be dismissed. It may be pointed out, for example, that in 1 Corinthians 13:13 faith and hope 'abide' as well as love, and there is room for the supposition that the 'riches of Christ' are eternally unsearchable and are waiting to be eternally explored in this spirit of faith and hope. But all this is very far from an intermediate state of penal

LIFE 2: THE SEQUEL

discipline such as 'purgatory', and if Bicknell meant the one he should not have called it the other.[8]

Calvary or Purgatory?

Purgatory means penal suffering. In its Roman homeland it teaches that individual Christians must to a large extent bear their own sin. The blood of Christ, it is taught, cleanses all sin at baptism; but thereafter, far from leaving the burden down, pilgrims must shoulder their own pack and fend for themselves. Calvary is but the halfway house to salvation. Every doctrine of Purgatory, however refined, must by definition share this belittlement of the Cross.

The satisfied God

The question, therefore, arises: *how* sufficient is the death of Christ? Does it deal with the problem of sin in whole or only in part?

There is a time-honoured and wonderful description of the Cross, which cannot be bettered: *The Finished Work of Christ*. This means three things: firstly, that the Holy God Himself requires nothing more to be done for the salvation of sinners than that His Son died for them. Paul teaches this in a graphic way when he depicts those who are saved as *already* seated with Christ in the heavenly places,[9] taken there with Him when God raised Him from the dead. By

---

[8] Addis, *Dictionary*, as above, rests the case for Purgatory on '… general principles of Scripture rather than … particular texts often alleged in proof' (p. 689), but the 'general principles' are in fact verses like 1 John 3: 2f. which refer to Christian growth in holiness in this life, a truth which is not in dispute but which no more bears on the matter in question than does Bicknell's reasoning.

[9] Ephesians 2:1-10. Believers do not reach heaven by a process which started at Calvary (and which, were it so revealed, could include Purgatory). Strictly speaking we reached heaven at the very moment Christ died. Cf. A. M. Stibbs, *The Finished Work of Christ*, IVP 1954; J. R. W. Stott, *The Cross of Christ*, IVP, 1986, passim and pp. 87-163.

this we are helped to see the Cross through God's eyes: the death of Christ is such a sufficient thing that as far as the Holy God is concerned nothing more remains to be done. Our whole salvation has been secured by the Cross and, at the very moment of the Cross, the whole redeemed community was, there and then, welcomed and eternally established in His presence.

The seated Priest
Secondly, when we speak of the finished work of Christ we mean that there is nothing more Christ can do for the salvation of sinners. Here we may take as proof a fact which means so much in the epistle to the Hebrews: Jesus the Priest 'when he had offered one sacrifice for sins for ever, sat down at the right hand of God; from henceforth waiting till his enemies be made the footstool of his feet ...' (10:12f.). To sit down signifies the completion of the work; to await the submission of foes means that they are already defeated. In these two ways all the objective conditions of salvation have been fulfilled by the death of Christ: the position of the seated Priest at God's right hand symbolizes that He has been welcomed back by the Father and that His work of salvation has been fully accepted. God is fully satisfied by what His Son has done. Furthermore, there is no foe left to defeat; all have been already overcome.

In the third place we come to subjective factors: there is nothing more which sinners require to be done to meet their need: their sins are all fully forgiven (Eph. 4:32; Col. 2:13); we now enjoy peace with God (Rom. 5:1; Eph. 2:16ff.; John 20:19f.); Jesus Christ is both our guilt offering and the bearer of our penalty (Isa. 53:4-6, 8, 10; Heb. 9:28; 1 Pet. 2:24); already, by the will of God, we stand 'sanctified by the offering of the body of Jesus Christ *once-for-all*' (Heb. 10:10).

'Qualified'

All this unvarying New Testament truth is summed up in one wonderful passage in Colossians 1:12-14. Here is salvation subjectively stated – 'we have redemption, the forgiveness of sins'; here is salvation objectively secured – God 'rescued us from the dominion of darkness and brought us into the kingdom of the Son of his love'; and here is salvation eternally effective – the full satisfaction of God with what He accomplished in the work of Christ by which He 'qualified us to be partakers of the inheritance of the saints' (Col. 1:12). The whole work of salvation is cast into the past; it rests upon Calvary; there is no future note sounded in this passage. We have been qualified, and nothing remains to be done. Purgatory is excluded.

'Finished' means 'Finished'

The centrality of Calvary underlines the scriptural affirmation that without the shedding of blood there is no remission of sin (Heb. 9:22). Where then are the fires of Purgatory? The blood of Christ is all-sufficient and leaves nothing undone, cleansing us from all sin (1 John 1:7).

And if, on the grounds that the saving work of Christ is *really* finished, Purgatory must be denied, then for the same reason we must dismiss its ecclesiastical fellow-traveller, 'the requiem celebration of the Holy Communion'. The word 'finished', understood in its biblical significance as outlined above, not only excludes any supposed repetition of the Cross, but also any proposed prolongation, re-enactment, re-presentation, or what you will. We are taught that what Jesus did on the Cross was accomplished 'through the eternal Spirit' – it was a single act with everlasting consequences. It originated in and perfectly matched the will of God the Father, was effectuated by God the Holy Spirit and accomplished totally and finally by the sacrifice of God the Son. There are no grounds for holding that Christ Himself is now occupied in re-presenting Calvary before the throne of God. A correct understanding of the blessed hope of everlasting life restores to us a correct enjoyment of the Lord's Supper as a 'memory of that his precious death',[10] but itself not in any sense a sacrifice whether for the living or for the dead.

Prayers for the dead?

But however firmly we reject the idea of Purgatory,[11] one would need to be insensitive to a degree to be unaware of the cry of the bereaved heart for some continuing relationship with departed loved ones, and the question naturally arises: can we not even pray for them?

Progress and regress[12]

Even a cursory glance through the Book of Common Prayer, noting in passing the deep feeling expressed, for example, in the Litany, the Visitation of the Sick, or in the Burial Service itself, will acquit the Reformers and the framers of this liturgy of any charge of insensitivity to human need. Nevertheless they rejected prayers for the dead.

---

[10] The Book of Common Prayer, Service of Holy Communion. Cf. S. Motyer, *Remember Jesus*, Christian Focus Publications, 1995.

[11] We need to beware of the abandonment of the name but the retention of the idea. Bicknell, as above, notes that the name, Purgatory, 'has evil associations and is perhaps best avoided' but goes on to quote Hort who objected to the name but retained for the dead a period of chastening discipline on the ground that 'it seems incredible to me that the divine chastisements should in this respect change their character when this visible life is ended'.

[12] Maybe I ought to apologise that this section is so heavily 'Anglican'. This was, however, not only the easiest way for me to deal with the subject, but inevitable in the light of the original objective of this book. The practice of 'prayers for the dead' is, however, widespread in the denominations, and the arguments here, Anglican in orientation, apply to all equally.

In the first Prayer Book of 1549, under the heading of a prayer 'for the whole state of Christ's Church', there was thanksgiving for the examples of the Virgin Mary, Patriarchs, Prophets and Apostles, and a commending to the mercy of God of His departed servants, with the request that they might receive 'everlasting peace'. All this was entirely omitted in the second Book of 1552, and (significantly) the title of the prayer was altered to read 'for the whole state of Christ's Church militant here in earth'.[13]

It was not until the Book of Common Prayer of 1662 that this prayer was extended to include a thanksgiving for departed Christians, coupled with prayer that we may share the glory with them hereafter. And even this mild addition was a matter of considerable controversy at the time.

In the light of this it is indeed remarkable that the Lambeth Conference Report of 1958 can summarize the history of praying for the departed in the Church of England, by saying that 'our Church formularies deliberately leave room for both ... points of view'.[14] The wish must be father to the thought. Rather, the exclusion of this type of prayer would not seem to indicate that the Reformers intended the question to remain open.[15]

---

[13] E.g. *The First and Second Prayer Books of Edward VI*, Everyman, London, 1910, pp. 221ff., 382.

[14] *The Lambeth Conference 1958*, London, 1958, Section 2. Para. 93.

[15] R. P. Blakeney, *The Book of Common Prayer, Its History and Inter-pretation*, London 1865, pp. 389f.; Neil and Willoughby, *The Tutorial Prayer Book*, London 1912, pp. 317., 481ff.; D. E. W. Harrison, *The Book of Common Prayer,* London 1946, p. 116, 'The medieval Catholic prayed for all the dead except the Saints, for Purgatory was the common expectation of all men. The Reformers, finding no scriptural warrant for such prayers, removed them from the public worship of the Church.' This is very exact. If the Lambeth Bishops felt that deliberate removal implies a desire to leave the matter open, all rational discourse ceases.

Lambeth 1958, however, seems to have had something of a *penchant* for finding open questions, for its judgment on the attitude of Scripture to praying for the dead was equally unsatisfactory. Since the canonical Scriptures give no instruction, nor even plain hint[16] that we are to pray for the dead, and yet are full of teaching, implication and example on every other sort of prayer, how is it possible to say that 'the evidence from this source does not amount to conclusive proof in either direction', and leave it at that? Even if Scripture were to be judged 'not conclusive', the balance of its evidence would still be entirely on the one side and not on the other.

Error restored

The Lambeth bishops were, however, a faithful mirror of the Anglican scene, for the reintroduction of prayers for the dead has been one of the features of this century: the Scottish Episcopal Church adopted them into its liturgy in 1912, and the Protestant Episcopal Church of the USA followed suit in 1928. As is well known, prayers for the dead, along with 'Reservation of the Sacrament', was one of the storm-centres in the Prayer Book crisis of 1928 in the Church of England. Since then prayers of this type have passed into common use in the Established Church.

For further evidence of the mind of the Reformers, see *The Book of Homilies*, London 1852, where the homily concerning prayer (p. 309) condemns prayer for the dead because of lack of scriptural warrant, because of the decisiveness of this life and because (there being no Purgatory) the dead are either in paradise where they do not need our prayers or under divine judgment in which case our prayers are of no avail.

[16] Appeal to 2 Timothy 1:16f. is customary in justification of praying for the dead. We know nothing, however, about the facts behind this verse – even whether Onesiphorus was dead! The argument would not be from silence but from ignorance.

In 1928 the rejection of the revised Prayer Book by Parliament turned out to be the winning of a battle, not of the war. The adverse parliamentary vote was rendered ineffective by an official declaration by the bishops that they would not consider the use of the 1928 book as inconsistent with the principles of the Church of England. Following this intentional encouragement to break the law, what was gained in the Commons was lost in a long process of attrition until, today, prayers for the dead are explicitly provided in the Alternative Services Book and in more recent Common Worship.[17]

Resignation

Superficially, one particular type of prayer for the dead which seems legitimate, human and innocuous is the prayer resigning the soul, immediately after death, to God. To consider it briefly will focus our attention on the problems and unexpected pitfalls of such prayers.

For whom?

In the first place, for whom are we praying? Is the object of our prayer a believer or a declared unbeliever or a person about whose spiritual state we are ignorant. Few will urge that we have warrant to pray for the unbeliever: there are too many verses of Scripture pointing to this life as the sole opportunity of faith in Christ, too many references to the dread possibility of 'dying in sin' (for example John 3:36; Heb. 9:27; Ezek. 3:18ff.; John 8:21, 24). Here, at least, is an area where to pray would be to abuse the gift of prayer, making it contradict what God has revealed.[18]

---

[17] W. Joynson-Hicks, *The Prayer Book Crisis,* Putnam, 1928; C. S. Carter and A. Weeks, *The Protestant Dictionary,* Harrison Trust, 1933, art., 'The Prayer Book'.

[18] Cf., N. T. Wright, *For All The Saints,* pp. 48-54.

Reverent doubt

Concerning those whose spiritual state is uncertain, we do well to recognize that this is the point where we should exercise reverent doubt rather than believing prayer, for we have no basis of revealed truth on which to pray. E. B. Pusey well quotes P. Ravignan to the effect that 'at the last moment of its passage on the threshold of eternity, there occur doubtless divine mysteries of justice, but above all of mercy and love', and that 'we abstain from sounding (i.e. 'probing') indiscreetly the divine counsels, but we know indubitably that on each occasion they are worthy of God and of his infinite goodness as well as of his justice'.[19]

This is undoubtedly so, for God can never act out of character. It is His nature always to have mercy and if we, in our poor inadequate way would leave no stone unturned for the eternal welfare of those we love, we may be very certain that He who loves them even more will do no less. There is also this, that, according to His promise, God's Word will not return to Him without having accomplished what He intended (Isa. 55:8-11) and on this we may rely: that the truth of the gospel, heard perhaps in childhood, will leap into action at the moment of death. But we do not know this in the same way that we know that this world is the end of the soul's probation, and that outside of Christ there is no salvation.

What to ask?

And for those who die in Christ what shall we pray? In what words shall we resign them to God? Shall we ask that 'light perpetual' may shine upon them? But what does this mean? Does it mean anything? Are we making a prayer request at all? Or shall we ask that they may 'rest in peace'? But surely this is to call in question whether

---

[19] E. B. Pusey, *What is of Faith*, etc., as above, p. 16.

they are saved or not; it is to pray for the converted as though they were unconverted. 'We *have* peace with God, through our Lord Jesus Christ' (Rom. 5:1), and it can no more be asked on behalf of the departed Christian than it can be asked on behalf of the Christian still present here.

Justification
But here is the very heart of the matter: is Christ sufficient for salvation? Did He really finish the saving work at Calvary? The question of prayer for the dead is settled on the same ground as the question of Purgatory and requiem communions.

We have already noticed the confusion of thought which makes the situation after death relative to the progress of our sanctification here on earth. We cannot stress too carefully that the eternal destiny of Christians is related to the fact that, though sinners, we are justified sinners, already and unchangeably accorded the status before God of those who never sinned; we have been granted the imputed righteousness of Christ (Rom. 3:21-26; Phil. 3:9). Even while on earth we are seated with Christ in heaven (Eph. 2:4ff.), and how much more so when we have gone to be with Christ which is far, far better (Phil. 1:23)!

Very often we do not enter into the deepest comforts of Christian faith because we shy away from apparently harsh facts. Our believing departed do not need our prayers. The Lamb Himself is leading them to living fountains of waters; God has wiped away every tear from their eyes (Rev. 7:17). If we resort to praying *for* our dead, then we are denying the reality and efficacy of Christ's saving work; we are acting as though Calvary is insufficient.

Jesus and Stephen
There are two prayers of resignation in the New Testament. One is the prayer of Jesus (Luke 23:46). The other,

also made before death and prayed by a person for himself, is the prayer of Stephen (Acts 7:55-60), and it typifies for all Christians the confidence in the face of death which comes through knowing how complete is the victory of Christ. Inherent in Calvary is the exaltation of the Lord Jesus to the highest heaven, the throne of God. Philippians 2:9ff. is typical with its initial 'therefore' seeing the exaltation of Christ as the divine reaction to His voluntary death. Nothing less than this is the efficacy of the finished work of salvation wrought by Christ for every believer. The Son of man still stands on the right hand of God to receive His own into His eternal and immediately enjoyed glory.

The prayers which most suit Christian bereavement and which also breathe the deepest and surest comfort into the sad heart are prayers of thankfulness for the one we love, for the divine love which allowed us to love each other on earth, for the joys of heaven into which our beloved has already entered and for the joyful hope of reunion in the heavenly places.[20]

Appendix (1) **Those who have never heard**

I have been careful in this study of human destiny to restrict the discussion to two classes: those who have heard of and have accepted Christ, and those who have heard and rejected. But there is a third group: those who have never heard. What of them?

---

[20] N. T. Wright (pp. 74, 75) urges us to 'talk to God' about our loved ones who died in faith, and, in this light, rightly says 'there is no reason why prayer should... stop just because the person you are praying for happens now to be "with Christ, which is far better"', and he goes on to ask, 'Why not simply celebrate the fact?' Indeed! The problem, however arises when our prayers of celebration slip over into prayers of intercession. Even to ask 'May they rest in peace and rise in glory' (which Wright approves, pp. 75, 76) is as meaningless as the prayer about 'light perpetual'.

Conscience

On this point, there is, as far as I can see, no unequivocal teaching of Scripture and my position is one of reverent agnosticism. There may be a clue in Paul's teaching that 'when the Gentiles which have no law do by nature the things of the law these, having no law, are a law unto themselves; in that they show the work of the law written in their hearts' (Rom. 2:14-15). This passage, however, is in the setting of the topic of judgment, and suggests that those who have no revelation from God are judged by the light of nature and conscience.

This is certainly Paul's position in Romans 1 where he holds that humankind, simply because they are *human*, ought to have known better than to worship and serve the creature instead of the Creator, and are therefore culpable before God (Rom. 1:18-25). In the Old Testament, Amos, likewise, condemned Israel and Judah for infidelity to revelation, but the heathen nations around them for crimes against the voice of conscience (Amos 1:3–2:16).

But this line of reasoning only leaves it open to us to cry out: 'Who then can be saved?' For who has ever lived up to the light he has had – however meagre that light? And who indeed can possibly stand when God judges the secret heart (Rom. 2:16)?

Unconscious devotion?

James Denney held that the clue to the problem is our Lord's parable of the sheep and the goats: 'All the nations – all the Gentiles – are gathered before the King; and their destiny is determined, not by their conscious acceptance or rejection of the historical Saviour, but by their unconscious acceptance or rejection of Him in the persons of those who need services of love.'[21] This, again, may be so, but the

---

[21] J. Denney, *Studies in Theology*, London 1894, p. 243; but especially J. R. W. Stott, *Essentials* as above, p. 325.

parable hardly seems to warrant certainty, for, apart from the fact that it would appear to be salvation by works, the lost in the parable do seem to lay claim to a knowledge of Christ when they argue in their own defence, 'Lord, when did we see you ... ?' (Matt. 25:44).

Abraham's word
There is, in fact, only one ground of certainty for our feet. It is ancient, but it has matured with the years and with increasing light of revelation. The words are those of Abraham: 'Far be it from you to do such a thing – to kill the righteous with the wicked, treating the righteous and the wicked alike. Far be it from you! *Will not the Judge of all the earth do right?*' (Gen. 18:25).

While we may thus safely leave this matter with God, there are some remarks which seem important: firstly, our ignorance of the answer to this question does not permit us to draw negative conclusions about the uniqueness and finality of Christ and His religion, and the necessity of justification by faith. *We must not bring what is positively revealed into jeopardy because of something which is not revealed.*

There may be a facade of reasonableness to say, with W. R. Matthews, that 'the study of Comparative Religions has put our Christian faith in a new perspective', and that 'we know that there have been and are men of other faiths than ours who have loved God and brought forth fruits of the Spirit' and that because of these things we must revise the doctrine of Salvation in Christ alone.[22] Certainly, we

---

[22] W. R. Matthews, *The Thirty-Nine Articles*, Hodder and Stoughton, 1961, p. 28. Essentially the same mode of argument was used by the Sadducees as by Matthews. See Matthew 22: 23-33. Because they could not answer the problems involved in their cautionary tale about the seven brothers, they rejected plainly revealed truth. Very different in its scriptural integrity is Dr Stott's treatment of the subject in *Essentials*, as above, pp. 320-329.

cannot dismiss these men of other faiths, but neither can we sacrifice the exclusive claims of God Incarnate through our inability to see how God will deal with them. *Ignorance on one point does not justify abandonment of revealed truth on another.*

Possibilities

Three possibilities open up. The first is a straightforward denial of Scripture. This would involve noting that many really good people never had the chance to hear of Christ and therefore saying either that a chance must surely await them beyond the grave,[23] or else, going the whole hog, that 'everyone without any exception whatever has been redeemed by Christ ... With each man without any exception whatever Christ is in a way united, even when that man is unaware of it'.[24]

Secondly, J. N. D. Anderson represents a mediate position,[25] that where there are those who, out of self-despair, cry out for divine mercy, the merciful God credits to them the atoning work of His Son. Once again, however, what can we say but, 'who can tell?' for Scripture is silent – and certainly Anderson's appeal to the Old Testament sacrificial system in support of his position is of highly dubious validity.

This brings us full circle to where we started: *What is not revealed in Scripture we cannot know.* What we do know is that there is no salvation outside of Christ, that the Judge of all the earth will do right, that in Him there is an unfathomable well of abundant pardon and that in

---

[23] D. L. Edwards, *The Last Things Now*, as above, pp. 72-78.

[24] Pope John Paul II, *Lumen Gentium*, paragraph 14.

[25] J. N. D. Anderson ,*Christianity and World Religions: The Challenge of Pluralism*, IVP, 1984. But see also R. Dowsett, *God, that's not Fair!* IVP, 1985; M. Goldsmith, *What about other Faiths?* Hodder & Stoughton, 1989.

the end the redeemed will not be a meagre few but an innumerable company (Rev. 7:9).

Appendix (2): **Reincarnation**

Two very basic human intuitions lie behind all the many differences in detail that mark the theory that individual souls are reborn on earth in a succession of lives spread over great lengths of time: the first is that we are not yet ready for the perfect state and therefore need further time and more opportunity, and the second is that injustices and wrongs demand retribution which does not always seem to be exacted within one lifetime. In Hinduism, 'Karma is the underlying law of the universe, which no god or man can set aside. It is the law that whatever a man sows he must reap exactly'.[26]

Within this broad framework differences abound as between Plato in the past, Hinduism and Buddhism, past and present, and in our own day, Theosophy, Anthroposophy, Rosicrucianism and New Age thought. Yet even without delving further, a basic opposition between Holy Scripture and reincarnation has already emerged: Job spoke for the Bible when he affirmed that 'he who goes down to Sheol does not return' (7:9). This passage, of course, has in mind the dead coming back as the people they used to be to the homes where they used to live. Reincarnationists do not affirm this sort of return. The reincarnate appear at a different time and place, maybe in a different gender, possibly as a different species. But if Job's assertion is therefore too narrow, Hebrews 9:27 makes up the deficiency: 'Man is destined to die once, and after that to face judgment.' Any notion that this judgment might decide on the penal course of a return to live again on earth finds no support in the Bible.

---

[26] J. S. Wright, 'The Supposed Evidence for Reincarnation', *Journal of the Transactions of the Victoria Institute*, Vol. LXXXIII, 1951.

Three other lines of opposition between Scripture and Reincarnation can be noted briefly. First, on the one occasion when the Lord Jesus could have assented to reincarnation He did not do so. The disciples proposed it as a logical explanation why a man should have been born blind (John 9:2, 3) and Jesus rejected their explanation.

Secondly, some schools of reincarnation propose some future goal of perfection. Plato,[27] for example, used 'myths' to sketch out the hope that after due preparatory lives the individual might at last enter the world of the Forms and enjoy the vision of the Good, but, in common with all such views, he proposed a scheme of self-salvation. Is there anything the Bible rejects so roundly?

Thirdly, the Bible allows us real glimpses of people beyond the grave and always implicitly affirms the continuation of individuality and personality. David expected to meet his dead infant son in Sheol (2 Sam. 12:23); the Samuel of 1 Samuel 28:15 is identical with the man known throughout the book; even more significantly, after such a lapse of time, Moses and Elijah came as themselves to the Mount of Transfiguration (Luke 9:29, lit., 'two men who were Moses and Elijah'); best of all there is the risen life of the Lord Jesus Himself. He who is alive for ever more (Rev. 1:18) affirmed 'It is I myself' (Luke 24:39).

Buddhism, with its intricate understanding of reincarnation and its detailed disciplines for achieving ever higher incarnate forms, has as its supreme objective the progressive negation of personal individuality and the goal of Nirvana, absorption into Nothingness, like blowing out a candle flame.[28] But even if we were, *per impossibile,* to imagine that the resurrected Jesus was the end result of millennia of reincarnations, He turns out to be even

---

[27] D. L. Edwards, *Last Things,* as above, pp. 31-38; O. Guinness, *The Dust of Death,* IVP, 1973, pp. 215-220.

[28] D. L. Edwards, *Last Things,* p. 32.

more Himself than before! Even larger than life! And for ourselves, poetic exaggerations like Wesley's 'lost in wonder, love and praise' should be avoided: we shall be like Him (1 John 3:2, 3), the individual redeemed objects of His shepherding care (Rev. 7:9-17), our names recorded in His book (Rev. 5:1; 20:15) and our personalities both hallowed and secured by the seal of His ownership and recognition (Rev. 22:4).

In the paper quoted above, J. S. Wright investigates evidence brought forward in favour of reincarnation, that individuals claim knowledge of their previous lives and even verifiable details about earlier times which seem not to have become available to them by ordinary means.[29] This is a huge subject, involving as it does very mysterious dimensions of the human psyche, in particular, perhaps, the relation of the unconscious mind to the dimensions of space and time.

Wright's conclusion, however, seems sound that such 'recollections' are so few and far between that it is a more scientific course to relate them to the known (even if not wholly understood) evidence of comparable powers. He notes in particular that some (equally few, certainly) have an ability to see the future and that others (again few) can engage in psychometry – by handling an object they tell facts about the past (and future) of its owner. His paper records one of his correspondents (Dr B. F. C. Atkinson) as urging also the possibility of satanic/demonic activity. Wright basically accepts this, but at the same time hesitates in 'using Satan as a *deus ex machina*.'

---

[29] J. Blanchard, *Whatever happened*, as above, pp. 86-88.

6

THE COMMUNION OF SAINTS

For the person who dies the sting of death is sin (1 Cor. 15:56), the certainty of personal unfitness to appear before a holy God; but for the bereaved the sting of death is separation. Christians acknowledge this, as often, in prospect of the death of a loved one, they say: 'I know it is better to be with Christ; but I dread the separation.' Without any loss of Christian certainty as to the life after death, many would join Tennyson's 'In Memoriam' in the cry 'for the touch of a vanished hand, and the sound of a voice that is still'.

Indeed, among the euphemisms for death, none is more true than to say: 'He is gone.' And while many have found a not inadmissible comfort in the look of peace on the face of their beloved dead, a truer description of the appearance of the dead is emptiness. One who used to live here has now departed – to be with Christ, to be much better off – and we are left. The contact of the years has been severed in a second, and cannot be recalled.

Spiritualism

Or can it be? Is there nothing retrievable? Cannot some contact be established even if things will never be quite the same again? It is at this point that we meet the claims of Spiritualism to overleap the gap between this world and the world of spirits and to bring together again those whom death has divided. To some the motive may be sheer curiosity about the other side of death, but to many it is the ache of bereavement and the longing for a loved one. Is this contact with the spirit-world allowable? The question is not a light one; it embraces much of the world's heartache. If contact is possible and permissible then it would be criminal to withhold it. But is it? Consider the following facts.

The Claims of Christ

Spiritualism as a system challenges the exclusive claims of Christ. It may have room for a Jesus who was a superior medium, but it has no room for Jesus Christ as the New Testament describes Him. Certainly, He is no longer the sole Mediator between God and Man (1 Tim. 2:5), for His place is taken by a host of 'spirit guides' or 'spirit-controls' speaking through a human medium. These are known by names: 'Pheneas, the spirit guide of Sir Arthur Conan Doyle ... Lily, the guide of Lady Doyle; and, at the present time (1942) White Hawk, the guide of the "Tottenham Healer": Lone Wolf of Neil Arnauld of Hampstead ...'[1]. But, as Bede Frost later writes, 'it is clear that Spiritist belief in Jesus Christ is not that of Christians; nor, so far as I know, have they dared to assert that messages have been received from him.'[2]

---

[1] B. Frost, *Some Modern Substitutes for Christianity*, Mowbray, 1942, p. 70.

[2] Frost, as above, p. 71.

By the same token, the Lord Jesus has lost His claim to be the final revelation of God. We recall that He asserted His sole competence to declare the 'heavenly things' because He alone came down from heaven (John 3:12, 13). How mistaken He was! There are many, it would appear, who can reach up to heaven, the 'mediums', and many who can come down, the 'guides'. The Lord Jesus is thus marginal to spiritualism, and is certainly not God, as the New Testament declares Him to be.

'Two fundamental beliefs – the deity of Christ and the forgiveness of sin through his atoning death are denied by almost all the messages bearing on this subject that profess to come from advanced spirits ... Lord Dowding, one of the most fervent modern propagandists for Spiritualism, says, towards the end of his book *Modern Mansions*: "The first thing which the orthodox Christian has to face is that the doctrine of the Trinity seems to have no adherents in advanced circles of the spirit world. The divinity of Christ as a co-equal partner with the Father is universally denied. Jesus Christ was indeed the Son of God, as also are we sons of God ... (Christians) are taught to believe in the remission of sins to the penitent, through the virtue of Christ's sacrifice and atonement. This doctrine Imperator (that is, the spirit-control) vigorously combats in a score of passages".'[3]

---

[3] J. O. Sanders and J. S. Wright, *Some Modern Religions*, IVP, 1956, pp. 35-36; H. Porter, *The Challenge of Spiritualism*, Faith Press, 1938, p. 11, quotes a spiritualist 'adaptation' of the hymn 'Come, let us join our cheerful songs':

'No sin-atoning sacrifice
Can banish grief and woe;
But manfully we learn to live
By reaping what we sow.'

Uncertainty

The second fact is that Spiritualism, for all its facade of 'evidence', is full of uncertainty. For one thing, too many frauds have been exposed in the past for the inquirer ever again to be certain that he is not being duped.[4] This is not to deny that there are mediums; it is simply to affirm that the ordinary inquirer can never be certain. Were a Spiritualist to counter by saying that there have been and are many fraudulent clergy, the charge could only be admitted, but the cases are not similar. For in Christianity we are not subject to spiritual dictatorship. The Scriptures lie open for all to read. We do not invite people into the darkness of a seance, but into the light of an open Bible. Each can judge.

But even where there is no deliberate imposture, there is still uncertainty. When a medium speaks in the name of a departed relative, and offers some facts which are intended to identify the dead person, there is no certainty that this information is not derived from the inquirer by telepathy rather than by real contact with the spirit world: it might simply be an exercise in reading the minds of the living. One medium has put it on record that she draws the information which enables her to build the representations of the dead from the subconscious minds of inquirers.[5] And even could we dispose of this possibility and guarantee real, unimpeachable contact with the other world, who can tell that it is the spirit of the dear departed who speaks, and not some other spirit? Satan can transform himself into an angel of light (2 Cor. 11:14), and why should he not thus delude the living and keep them from the true knowledge of God in Christ?

---

[4] J. von Baalen, *The Chaos of the Cults,* Grand Rapids, 1948, pp. 31ff.; L. E. Froom, *Spiritualism Today*, Washington, 1963, p. 37.

[5] Sanders and Wright, as above, pp. 37, 38.

Spiritual danger

This raises the third fact which we must face about Spiritualism: its great danger. The severe warnings against consulting 'familiar spirits' or using 'necromancy' in the Old Testament, cannot have been issued for nothing (Lev. 19:31; 20:6; Deut. 18:10f; 26:14; Isa. 8:19; etc.). The Bible teaches the reality of Satan, the personal spiritual power of evil (Matt. 12:24-28; John 8:44; 12:31; 2 Cor. 4:4; Eph. 2:2; etc.); it also speaks of hosts of wicked spirits of great potency (Eph. 6:12; Matt. 25:41; etc.); it gives warning of deceiving spirits (1 John 4:1-3; 2 Cor. 4:4; cf. 11:13-15); and it instances demon possession (Matt. 4:24; 12:24ff.; Mark 1:23ff.; 5:2-13; Luke 9:1 with 10:17; etc.). Spiritualism can offer no safeguards against any of these – any more indeed than can the 'New Age' assumption that the spiritual reality that surrounds us in this world is wholly beneficial and benevolent! Add to them our own natural bent towards evil, and it is not possible to deny that 'every passive condition into which anyone puts himself is a door opened to the devil'.[6]

In addition to all these things, there is a difference between Spiritualism – and New Ageism – and Christianity which could easily be overlooked, but which is basic. The one is man-centred, the other God-centred. The spiritualists start with their own sense of loss; they allow all to be subordinated to the necessity to prolong *human* contact; they deliver themselves into the hands of a medium; they offer, as their crowning contribution, proof of *human* survival of death. The signpost points to humans all the time: their needs, their competence to meet them, their conquest of death. But Christianity points solely to the Lord Jesus Christ, to *His* conquest, to the reality of *His* safekeeping of loved ones, and to the hope of *His* personal coming again.

---

[6] J. Maritain, quoted by Frost, as above, p. 78.

The Resurrection

The resurrection of the Lord Jesus rests on the individual and cumulative significance of five well-attested facts.

First, the tomb was empty, a fact of such potency that even the Lord's enemies were shocked into perpetrating an attempted fraud (Matt. 28:11-15). Secondly, the body disappeared and was never even alleged to be 'found' – though this was the explanation which occurred to Mary Magdalene (John 20:13-15). No tomb-robbing could account for it, and all the more so when, in the third place, there is the evidence of the grave-clothes (John 20:7), 'the actual grave clothes, still lying in their original folds, untouched by human hands yet no longer containing the crucified body'.[7] Only the work of God can explain this. Fourthly, Christ appeared to His disciples, not as a 'ghost' from the dead, but as Himself, capable of being handled and touched, flesh and bones, the Jesus of old (Luke 24:36-43). And, fifthly, these appearances of Christ wrought a moral and spiritual transformation in those who saw Him: (contrast Luke 22:54-62 with Acts 4:13; John 20:19 with Acts 17:6). Is this the usual result of a seance?[8]

There is a sequence in these five points: the evidence of the empty tomb is reinforced by the disappearance of the body; this is in turn lifted to the plane of the supernatural by the state of the grave-clothes; the message of the grave-clothes is fulfilled in the appearances – 'the Lord is risen indeed' (Luke 24:34); and the objectivity and power of the risen Christ is displayed in the transformation and empowering of the apostles.

---

[7] R. V. G. Tasker, *The Gospel according to John*, IVP, 1960, p.221.

[8] A. T. Schofield, *Modern Spiritism*, Kessinger Pubs, 2003, 'A friend whose brother was one of the best-known spiritists in America told me that his brother did not know a single case where the study had been pursued without distinct deterioration of physical, mental or spiritual faculties.'

It is this fact – 'He is risen' – which the New Testament offers as the guarantee of life after death. One of the problems which Paul faced in the Corinthian Church was the disposition to doubt, even deny, the resurrection of the dead. In refutation of this, however, he offers no seance-experience. He does not point to the dead but to Christ: 'If Christ is preached that he has been raised from the dead, how can some of you say that there is no resurrection of the dead?' (1 Cor. 15:12). And at the other end of his argument, as against the opinion that 'those also who have fallen asleep in Christ are lost', he replies triumphantly: "But now Christ has been raised from the dead' (1 Cor. 15:20).

In respect to our dead, then, there is a reality of departure. They are gone, and we can do ourselves nothing but mischief by trying to have it otherwise, for we will either tumble headlong into spiritualist danger or relapse into the twilight to which Queen Victoria delivered herself – the half-life of the unsurrendered past. They are gone, but also they have arrived. Look at Christ. He is the proof; He is the guarantee. Acquaint yourself with the Living Lord. Our departed fellow-Christians are with Him, and it is far, far better.

Oneness in Christ

But what of 'the communion of saints'? How are we still one with those who have gone on?

There are two aspects of this: we and they are one in Christ, and one in expectation of Christ.

A sort of comparison can be drawn in respect of Christians who have gone to the other side of the world in Christ's service. Our continuing oneness with them is entirely Christ-centred: there is oneness in loving the same Lord, in continuing to love one another with that characteristic love which only Christians know, and, since they and we are still in the body, there is oneness of mutual concern issuing in prayer. This is indeed a 'communion of the saints' and, apart from the last matter, our oneness with departed Christians is exactly the same. Those who realize this find it a high point of experience when 'with Angels and Archangels, and with all the company of heaven, we laud and magnify Thy glorious name, evermore praising thee, and saying: Holy, Holy, Holy Lord God of hosts, heaven and earth are full of thy glory: Glory be to thee O Lord most High'.[9] Are we praying for our dead here? Certainly not. Are we in their presence or they in ours? Certainly not. Are we one with them in praising one glorious God? Assuredly we are.

In the interim
There is also oneness of expectation. We are told very little of the details of the state of our dead in Christ. We know that they have left the body behind, and we know that it is far, far better, as they are in the Lord's presence.

This topic will occupy our attention more fully in the next chapter, but for the moment we must try to understand what is usually called the 'intermediate state'. We have already seen that Scripture will not allow us to think of any form of Purgatory, nor will it admit of any 'second chance' for those who here have rejected Christ. Nevertheless we on earth cannot picture our dead otherwise than as waiting for that final glory, which will be theirs and ours at the return of Christ.

Admittedly, all talk of 'waiting' and of an 'intermediate state' reflects the limitations of earthly processes of thought. We are creatures of time, and we can think only of eternity as 'endless time', whereas it is an entirely different mode of existence altogether. The very phrase

---

[9] *The Book of Common Prayer,* Service of Holy Communion.

'intermediate state' suggests that beyond the grave there is a time-sequence parallel to ours, which will, with ours, terminate at the Second Coming. This is an insufficient way of thinking but no other is at our disposal. Already our dead in Christ belong to eternity. However, rather than speculate or philosophize at this point, it is better to confine ourselves to the language of Scripture.

Waiting

Two observations are important: in the book of Revelation we are shown the souls of Christian martyrs, 'under the altar' crying out, 'How long, Sovereign Lord' (6:9, 10). We are, of course, dealing with a pictorial representation of their state. 'Under the altar' signifies that their place in heaven has been secured by the sacrifice of Christ. The cry 'How long?' depicts them as longing for the consummation, when all God's people will be avenged and gathered. Consequently, we are justified in speaking of a time of 'waiting', but we must accept that this too may be a pictorial representation necessitated by our limitations. Eternity itself alone will reveal what eternity is.

At any rate, the great event of the Second Coming will terminate the heavenly 'waiting', just as it consummates the hope of the Church on earth. The Second Coming effects as real a change for those who have died as for those who remain alive, for we read that 'the dead in Christ shall rise first' (1 Thess. 4:16).

Once again, our thinking about our dead must be Christ-centred. The communion of saints includes one-ness of expectation that He will come and gather His own, so that 'we that are alive, that are left, shall *together with them* be caught up in the clouds, to *meet the Lord in the air*' (1 Thess. 4:17).

Aspects of the Return

The Lord's Second Coming and our gathering to Him will take place 'in the clouds ... in the air' (1 Thess. 4:17). This double expression is full of meaning. In the Bible the cloud and the clouds symbolize the real, personal presence and glory of God (Exod. 13:20-22; 14:19, 24; 19:16-18; 24:15-18; Ps. 99:7; Luke 9:34-35). When Jesus comes again we will be gathered into the very presence of God to experience the full reality of the fact that we have 'received reconciliation' (Rom. 5:11) through the death of Jesus and that He died 'the just on behalf of the unjust that he might bring us to God' (1 Pet. 3:18).

The Return thus consummates the atoning work of the Cross; but it also consummates the victory of the Cross, for 'the air' is the locus of the princedom of Satan (Eph. 2:2). We are thus drawn right into the usurped dominion to meet at long last the Victor whose right it is to reign.

Visible actuality

The symbolic significance, however, of 'clouds' and 'air' is neither their whole meaning nor their first meaning. The Lord will return 'in the same way you have seen him go into heaven' (Acts 1:11), that is, personally and visibly, moving through the heavens (cf. Heb. 4:14).

To say this only recapitulates what He Himself taught (Mark 13:26; Luke 21:17), and if there are those who are disposed to urge that such an expectation falls below the intellectual and scientific sophistication of the present day, they ought to reflect that there is no argument against the Second Coming as Scripture describes it that could not equally be levelled, in its own terms, against the First Coming. Can contemporary sophistication come to terms with God as an infant, born of a virgin? Yet it was so!

Scripture offers us an expectation worthy of the returning Lord Jesus. Personally, visibly (Matt. 24:30), clothed with power and majesty (Rev. 1:7), awesome in holiness (Rev. 6:12-17), resplendent in glory (Mark 13:26), the same Jesus (Acts 1:11) who ascended will descend, and as by a spiritual magnetism those who are His will rise delightedly to meet Him and so shall they ever be with the Lord (1 Thess. 4:13-17).

Present hope

Of course, it may be God's will for any one of us to join our departed ones in the Lord's presence by death, to return with Him in His train (1 Thess. 3:13; 4:14) and to be united with our rising, resurrection bodies (1 Thess. 4:16). But Scripture would direct us rather to fill our eyes with the hope of His coming, and to rejoice even now in expectation of the fulness of glory and joy that will be His and, through Him, ours at that great day.

7

CHRISTIAN EXPECTATION

One of the most difficult things to keep constantly before our minds is the Bible's view of the *darkness* of this world. Of course, when we face a calamity, or when we view the plight in which many people live, we acknowledge that all is not well. But, by and large, we find life sweet and call death an unwelcome intruder, an enemy. We have good reason for doing so, and the Bible does so as well (1 Cor. 15:26). Nevertheless, the Bible encourages a different and truer perspective when it says 'the night is far spent' (Rom. 13:12), for the presence of sin and rebellion against God, and all the dire consequences of sin, broken lives, shattered hopes, war, suffering and cruelty, indeed make this world a dark and darkening place. It is against the background of this darkness that the brightness of the glory beyond the grave shines out.

Perspective
Picture it like this: a person sits reading at a window on an autumn afternoon. As the light fades, so the eyes

accustom themselves to the gloom and the reader reads on. But now another person comes into the room and switches on the light. 'What are you doing reading in the dark?' says the one; 'But I didn't realize how dark it was!' replies the other. So we may understand Paul when he tells us that the night (the present world) is far spent, and the day (the coming of Christ) is at hand (Rom. 13:12). We may not always realize the darkness now, but wait till we look back from the point of view of *that* day! 'The light of the moon shall be as the light of the sun, and the light of the sun shall be sevenfold, as the light of seven days, in the day when the LORD binds up the hurt of his people, and heals the stroke of their wound' (Isa. 30:26).

'To die is gain' (Phil. 1:21)

This is the perspective, too, in which we must view our own death: it also is a move from darkness into light, a completely gainful experience. Paul sums it up: 'To me, to live is Christ, and to die is gain' (Phil. 1:21), the 'gain' being the fuller knowledge and experience of Christ that death will bring.

In 2 Timothy 4:6 he enlarges the picture by suggesting all the delights of a long-delayed homecoming. This is the last of his letters, written when he felt the hour of death to be close. He describes it as 'the time of my departure', using a word (*analusis*) meaning either 'time for me to strike camp' or 'my time to weigh anchor'. Is the old tentmaker (Acts 18:3) using a picture drawn from his trade, or is the missionary traveller recalling many a past moment? In either case the substantial meaning is the same: all the discomforts and deprivations of the camping life and all the homesickness of the foreign land are now past.

Handley Moule, adopting the second of these meanings, caught the apostle's feeling exactly:

That delightful moment when the friendly flood heaves beneath the freed keel, and the prow is set straight and finally toward the shore of *home*, and the Pilot stands on board, at length 'seen face to face'. And lo, as he takes the helm, 'immediately the ship is at the land whither they go' (John 6:21).[1]

Planned fearlessness

Death is not so much something which happens to Christians as something God works for them. The death of the Christian is 'precious' to God (Ps. 116:15), something He prizes, like a jewel a lover gives with delight to a beloved. It is not a haphazard, chance thing, but a gift He bestows, His last and greatest earthly blessing. Psalm 23 displays this truth: the child of God is guided in 'paths of righteousness' (v. 3), that is, paths which are right, paths which make sense to God. This great statement of faith is bracketed on the one side (vv. 1-3a) by life's pleasantness: the green pastures and still waters, times of refreshment – all the bounties into which God lovingly guides His own. But on the other side (v. 4), with equally loving care, the hand of the Shepherd leads to 'the valley of the shadow of death',[2] and in that valley there is the immediate presence

---

[1] H. C. G. Moule, *The Second Epistle to Timothy,* London, 1905, p. 140, see also p. 159. D. Guthrie, *The Pastoral Epistles,* IVP, 1957, p. 169 supports the two possible references of *analusis,* either loosing moorings or striking camp. See also J. N. D. Kelly, *The Pastoral Epistles,* A. & C. Black, 1963. E. K. Simpson, however, (*The Pastoral Epistles,* IVP, 1954), acknowledges 'the allusion to unbinding' but prefers to leave the word to 'signify death itself, like our term "dissolution".' C. S. Lewis, *The Last Battle,* Fontana, 1982, p.172, 'No fear...' said Aslan. 'Have you not guessed ...(A)ll of you are – as you used to call it in the Shadowlands – dead. The term is over: the holidays have begun. The dream is ended: this is the morning.'

[2] The word should be rendered 'deep darkness' without excluding the particular 'deep darkness' of death where the context points to it.

of the Lord Himself; 'you are with me'. As the darkness deepens, the 'he' of verses 1-3a becomes the more personal 'you' of a close companion.

The sting drawn
Furthermore it is not only that the Lord's presence dismisses fear, but also that death itself has lost its sting. In order to appreciate this truth we need to remember the moral dimension of death. We naturally think of death in its physical aspects, the end of earthly life, the leaving behind of a body, and so forth. But death entered the world along with sin and can only cease when sin ceases. But here is our comfort: the Lord Jesus Christ has dealt with sin, and therefore death has lost its sting (1 Cor. 15:56, 57). Once more we are called to Christ-centred living: the more we see His atoning death as a 'full, perfect and sufficient sacrifice, oblation, and satisfaction for the sins of the whole world',[3] the more we cease to fear death.

Preparation
There are also other preparations for death, in addition to having the right attitude towards it. No matter how the mind accepts the blessedness of the Christian hereafter, the end of life on earth is a crisis, and only a fool will fail to prepare for it. For with death comes judgment, and the Christian is commanded so to live now as to be able to bear God's direct scrutiny then.

This does not contradict the Christian hope as we have tried to display it. Rather it is inseparable from the hope, because it is the Holy One Himself who is coming, and 'everyone who has this hope set on him purifies himself, even as he is pure' (1 John 3:3).

The parables of our Lord are very clear on this matter of judgment and preparedness. In the parable of the talents

---

[3] *The Book of Common Prayer,* Service of Holy Communion.

(Matt. 25:14-30), the departing master gave to his servants according to each one's ability, and when he returned, he inquired as to the profit made from the talents: i.e. was every ability fully and profitably used for Christ? In the parable of the pounds (Luke 19:11-27), however, each servant of the king received the same amount on deposit, and the returning king made it his first task to inquire into their use of his deposit: i.e. was the gospel, the common possession of all Christians, fully 'put to work' in evangelism? Again, in the parable of the ten virgins (Matt. 25:1-13), the coming of the bridegroom was a critical moment of truth, for the same shut door which safeguarded the eternal security of some barred the entrance of others. In the parable of the wedding feast (Matt. 22:1-13), the entrance of the king to see his guests put each on trial, and the one without the wedding-garment, the person whose merely formal testimony never resulted in a changed life (Rev. 19:9), was not accepted into the feast.

The Lord's parables do not, of course, teach that there are some Christians who will be excluded or ejected from the feast. The purpose of these parables is not to describe future scenes but, as indicated above, to underline what it is that distinguishes a real profession of faith from an unreal one, to enforce present truth. The bridesmaids all looked alike outwardly but there was a difference: some of them possessed also a hidden, inner reality of oil stored up. The sheep and the goats have identical implied professions of devotion to the King, but only the former served Him in meeting the needs of others.

The wedding feast story sums it all up: a genuine response to the invitation involves changing clothes (becoming a different person), the donning of that 'fine linen' which 'stands for the righteous actions of the saints' (Rev. 19:8).

Completing the sacrifice

For Paul this commitment of life, inwardly and outwardly, in devotion to Jesus continues right up to the very moment of death. This is what he means when he pictures dying as making a 'drink-offering': 'I am already being poured out' (2 Tim. 4:6). In the Old Testament sacrifices, the drink-offering was poured out on to the completed sacrifice.[4] So the Christian is called to live always as a sacrifice to the Lord (Rom. 12:1-2), with death as the final act of devotion and worship, the seal on a consecrated career.

Note how Paul goes on from this reference to death as a drink-offering first to look back over his consistent life: 'I have fought the good fight, I have finished the race, I have kept the faith.' Next he looks upward to the Judge: 'Henceforth there is laid up for me the crown of righteousness which the Lord the righteous Judge, will give to me at that day: and not only to me, but also to all them that have loved his appearing' (2 Tim. 4:7-8). His death will be his crowning act of obedience, completing his consecrated living ('good fight'), his unremitting service ('course'), and his faithfulness to the truth – the three modes of preparation indicated in our Lord's parables. On this basis, he will meet the Judge. Yet the crown is given not for success but for love of Him for whose appearing we long.

The Judgment Seat of Christ

The three main references to the judgment seat of Christ in the New Testament (Rom. 14:10; 1 Cor. 3:10-15; 2 Cor. 5:9ff.) fit in with all this and with the teaching drawn from the Lord's parables.

In the first place, the individual stands before Christ for judgment: 'each one' will receive 'what is due to him for the things done while in the body' (2 Cor. 5:10).

[4] A. Bonar, *A Commentary on the Book of Leviticus*, London, 1847, p. 37.

Secondly, judgment is given a different setting in each of the three passages. In Romans, the context is Christian relationships in a pagan society; in 1 Corinthians the metaphor of 'building' on the foundation of Christ, erecting a superstructure of thought, word and deed in harmony with such a foundation; and in 2 Corinthians, Paul proceeds from the judgment seat to the topic of evangelism and ambassadorship, indicating that here is an obligation about which Christ will inquire.

Assured salvation

But – we must say it again! – in all this searching inquiry, the salvation of the individual Christian is not for a moment in the slightest doubt, for, even though reward is related to our earthly character and conduct, salvation does not depend on our works but on the work of Christ. The dying thief is the exemplar of all the redeemed, as he proceeds from the death of sin directly to the bliss of paradise by simple faith in Christ (Luke 23:43), without the intervention of either a life of good works or the benefit of ceremony or sacrament. In the same way, when John sees all alike gathered before the throne of God, the redeemed are where they are by the blood of the Lamb (Rev. 7:9-17), and are preserved from wrath not by their own good works but by the inscription of their names in the Lamb's Book of Life (Rev. 20:12-15). Christians must live as those who will give an account, yet we can die as those whose eternal security is immediately certain: 'If any man's work shall be burned, he shall suffer loss: but *he himself shall be saved*' (1 Cor. 3:15).[5]

---

[5] This verse cannot allude to Purgatory (though, cf., *Catechism of the Catholic Church*, as above, section 1031). The 'fire' here 'tries'; that of Purgatory purifies; here it is works, not persons which are tried; the matter at issue is loss of reward at the last day, not purificatory suffering prior to the last day.

Falling asleep

The New Testament, however, focuses its chief attention rather on the benefits and blessings of the heavenly state.

The immediate state of the believer after death is often described as 'sleep': the Christian dead sleep in Jesus (1 Thess. 4:14), and the Lord Himself said that 'our friend Lazarus is fallen asleep' (John 11:11). But it is a metaphor, not a literal description.[6] The Bible speaks of things and states which are past our present comprehension, and, in order to make them intelligible to us, often uses pictures which appear to contradict each other.

For example, the relation which the Christian possesses towards God through Christ is sometimes called 'adoption as sons' and sometimes as 'becoming sons' (Eph. 1:5; John 1:12).[7] Logically, these are mutually exclusive states – for no-one can, in earthly terms, be both a natural and an adopted child. In Scripture each expresses an aspect of the truth – adoption calls attention to the basic fact of divine choice, bringing into the family someone who has no natural right or affiliation; sonship, on the other hand, takes note of the full reality of subsequent family membership and the child's sharing in the actual life of the Father.

So also, the 'sleep' metaphor must be balanced by those other descriptions which imply a conscious, living state. For example, to be 'absent from the body' is to be 'at home with the Lord' (2 Cor. 5:8) and, apparently, from the enthusiasm with which the apostle views it, to know and enjoy His company.

In the house of Jairus (Luke 8:49-56), the little girl was truly dead and the mourning party scoffed the Lord's

---

[6] For a contrary view, see E. W. Bullinger, *Selected Writings*, Bagster, 1960, pp. 107ff.

[7] O. Cullmann, *Immortality of the Soul or Resurrection of the Dead*, SCM, 1958, would appear to err here on the side of literalism.

assertion that she was asleep. There is the matter in a nutshell: to us the irreversible and tragic reality of death; to Him the simplicity of a touch and a word restoring wakefulness.

First Thessalonians 4:13-15 is something of a key passage in that it shows that 'sleep' refers to our observation of the moment of death and not to the subsequent state of those who have died. The Thessalonians were perturbed because they were seeing other Christians 'falling asleep' (present participle) before the Lord had yet come (v. 13). Paul offers them two assurances: first, in verse 14 that these Christians 'fell asleep' (aorist participle, of the past moment of death) 'through Jesus'. The force of the preposition 'through' (not 'in' as NIV) is that it is both 'through Jesus' that dying is transformed into dropping asleep and also that the whole experience of death – its timing included – is ordered 'through' Him. There is no such thing as an untimely death nor a Christian death that is anything other than falling asleep on earth to awake at once in His presence. Secondly, Paul offers the reassurance (v. 15) that those who 'fell asleep' (aorist participle, the earthly moment of dying) are priority participants in the Return.

Immediacy

Falling asleep on earth, the believer awakes at once to the presence of Christ in heaven. Paul does not himself refuse to die (Acts 25:11), knowing that 'to depart' (*analuo*, to strike camp; to cast off and sail) is 'to be with Christ'. The Lord Jesus when He comes will come 'with his saints' (1 Thess. 3:13), God will bring them 'with him' (1 Thess. 4:14) – for they are 'with him' already. Having enjoyed His presence ever since their heavenly awaking, they are the first to be gathered into the train of the returning Lord. It was in confirmation of this same truth that the Lord Jesus pledged to the 'dying thief' that 'Today you will be with me in Paradise (Luke 23:43).[8]

The resurrection body

The believers, then, are promised 'rest' from the toils and exactions of this life (Rev. 14:13), but our ultimate hope, while never losing this note of restfulness, is that we will receive from God the 'resurrection body'.

Using the metaphor of 'clothing', Paul speaks of three states: 'clothed', 'unclothed' and 'clothed upon'.[9] At death, the old clothing of the body is left behind, and the soul enters the rest of the Lord's immediate presence. Since, however, the soul is thus separated from its body, it is

---

[8] Bullinger, as above, dwells at length on this verse in order to show that the proper punctuation of the saying is 'I say to you today, You will be with me...'. His motivation is partly dogmatic, to allow the words to support his theory of soul-sleep immediately after death, but he urges a feature of the Greek text in support: the absence of the connective *hoti* ('that') after 'I say' and before 'You shall' proves that the temporal adverb 'today' should be connected back and not forward. This is extremely unsafe ground. The incidence or absence of *hoti* in New Testament Greek is unpredictable. Furthermore the cases where there is no *hoti* and the next word is an adverb or adverbial phrase are too few to establish a consensus. References like Matthew 16:2; 26:73 and Mark 7:6 show that the allocation of the adverb is a matter of contextual interpretation, not of linguistic usage. A. Plummer observes that to take 'today' with 'I say' 'robs it of almost all its force. When taken with what follows it is full of meaning' (*The Gospel according to St. Luke*, T & T Clark, 1896, p.535). N. Geldenhuys, '"Today" stands foremost because Jesus wishes to contrast the nearness of the promised happiness with the remote future to which the prayer of the thief refers' (*Commentary on the Gospel of Luke*, Marshall, 1956, p. 615). I. H. Marshall writes, '"Today" refers to the day of crucifixion as the day of entry into paradise' (*The Gospel of Luke*, Paternoster, 1978, p. 873).

[9] On the 'three states', L. Boettner, *Immortality*, Grand Rapids, 1956, pp. 96ff.; On 2 Corinthians 5:1-5, P. E. Hughes, *Paul's Second Epistle to the Corinthians*, Marshall, 1961; E. E. Ellis, *Paul and his Recent Interpreters*, Grand Rapids, 1961, pp. 35ff.; C. Hodge, *The Second Epistle to the Corinthians*, Banner of Truth, 1959.

'unclothed', a state as yet incomplete. But at His Second Coming and the accompanying great resurrection there is the new clothing, a body made to match the new life, when He 'fashions anew the body of our humiliation that it may be conformed to the body of his glory' (Phil. 3:21).

The metaphor of clothing has a long and rich history in the Bible. We can understand it with a simple question: Why does a girl wear a wedding dress at her wedding? Because she *is* a bride! The clothes display her nature (a bride) and her intention (to marry). In the same way the Lord showed Himself to Joshua as an armed man, displaying his nature as the victor and his intention to enter this fray and bring it to His appointed conclusion (Josh. 5:13–6:2ff.). As far as we are concerned, our natural body reflects, declares and serves the functions of our fallen nature: it is 'the body of our humiliation' and 'the body of this death' (Rom. 7:24). This is the body we lay aside when death 'unclothes' us and for a while, though with Christ and therefore 'far better', we remain unclothed. But perfection awaits; something much more wonderful lies ahead.

The image of God
Mankind was made 'in the image of God' (Gen. 1:26f.; 5:1), and God's purpose in redemption is to undo the damage and ruin of sin so that we may again display that image to the full. The present process of sanctification in the Christian is described as 'being renewed in knowledge in the image of its Creator' (Col. 3:10), and the end is that 'we shall be like him, for we shall see him as he is' (1 John 3:2).

God does not, of course, exist in an outward form, nor is visibility part of the divine essence. 'God is spirit' and no-one has ever seen God – by which we understand that God is not 'seeable' in His essential being (Exod. 33:20;

Isa. 31:3; John 1:18; 4:24; 1 Tim. 6:16). Nevertheless, in Scripture it says that various people did see God. Moses saw 'the form of God' (Num. 12:8); many others were granted visible manifestations of deity (Gen. 32:30; Judg. 13:22; Isa. 6:1), and the Lord Jesus said: 'Anyone who has seen me has seen the Father' (John 14:9). There is no contradiction. We can put it this way: though in His essential deity God is invisible, there is an outward form suited to His invisible glory.[10] It was in this outward form that God showed Himself from time to time.

Consequently when the Bible says that God 'created man in his image' it has the same meaning: that outward form which perfectly matches and expresses His inward essence or nature. In our case, of course, by the Creator's will, the visible outward expression is part of our essential constitution. 'Man' is an 'en-souled body' and an 'embodied soul', a psychosomatic unity. Therefore, redemption is not just 'saving the soul'; it is the full recovery, deliverance, renewal, re-creation and transformation of the whole person, body as well as soul, soul as well as body (Rom. 8:23; Phil. 3:20-21; 1 Thess. 5:23).

Continuity and transformation
Our present experience, however, is that the body militates against the living of the godly life. There is a downward drag in our bodily members (Rom. 7:18-23), whereby our best intentions and ideals are marred by the inability and rebellion of the body. How marvellous then is the promise of a body which will respond automatically to the promptings of God, and will be the perfect vehicle for the expression of the new nature! Yet it is the same body remade; it is the 'body of our humiliation', that is, the body which matches and expresses our fallen state, new-

---

[10] See J. A. Motyer, *Look to the Rock, An Old Testament Background to our Understanding of Christ,* IVP, 1996.

created by the returning Christ so that it will be like the body of His glory, the body of Jesus Himself in His risen ascended majesty.

Seed and flower
The relation of that resurrection body to the present body is one of both continuity and transformation: it will be related to the present body as a flower is to its own seed, and it will be as transformed as when a seed issues in a flower (1 Cor. 15:35-38, 42-44, 50-54).

This is Paul's illustration, but the experience of the Lord Jesus is an object lesson on the same topic. The risen Lord was wonderfully transformed so that powers were manifested in Him which hitherto He had not displayed. He was different to such an extent that sometimes He was not readily recognized (John 21:12). Yet He was the same Jesus as of old. When He took bread and broke it in the well-remembered way 'he was known by them in the breaking of bread', and when He came to the upper room He displayed Himself to their wondering and doubting eyes with the words: 'See my hands and feet, that it is I myself' (Luke 24:30-31, 39).

Recognition
Here, then, is the Bible's answer to the frequent question whether we shall recognize our loved ones in heaven. In terms of Paul's illustration, the wheat seed becomes the wheat ear, transformed and yet the same; in the Lord's experience, continuity of person – with consequent recognition by others – and yet wonderful transformation.

The rest of the Bible confirms this truth. Moses and Elijah appeared in glory at the Transfiguration hundreds of years after their departure from earth, but they were still the same people (Luke 9:32f.). If God is indeed 'the God of the living' then He is interested in Abraham, Isaac and Jacob as individual living entities, and (as we are told) we shall see them in the Kingdom (Luke 13:28).[11]

Of course, there is much here we cannot answer. Will those who died in infancy be infants still? Will grandparents still bear the marks of age? We are not told what the appearance of the resurrection-body will be, and we must fall back on Paul's illustration. The flower is the perfect maturity of the seed; the resurrection-body, as carefully chosen for each individual as the Master-Gardener has given each seed its 'body', will display the full maturity and perfection of each redeemed person's character in Christ.

Both 'Coming' and 'Rising' (1 Thess. 4:13-18)
Paul's dear Thessalonians were distressed that some of their number died before Christ came again. It was a natural reaction, for though they were aware that the only thing knowable about the date of the Coming is that no-one knows it (Mark 13:32; 1 Thess. 5:1) except the Father, yet Paul had rightly taught them to share his own imminent expectation. But what wonderful teaching their distress prompted! Their dead, already in Christ's presence, will come 'with him' (v. 14). But more: since at death they left part of themselves behind in the grave, they will be the first to rise (v. 16) for the great gathering. Thus Paul envisages the 'reconstitution' of the whole person, body and soul, in and with Christ, the union and 'clothing' of the redeemed soul with the resurrection body.

The glory of Christ
Even yet, however, we have not reached the climax of the heavenly blessedness. Beyond the joy of reunion and the

---

[11] J. R. W. Stott, *Christ the Controversialist*, IVP, 1970, pp. 49-64.

wonder of personal transformation, there is the glory of Christ Himself.

> The Bride eyes not her garments,
> But her dear bridegroom's face.
> I will not gaze on glory,
> But on my King of grace;
> Not on the crown he giveth,
> But his own pierced hand:
> The Lamb is all the glory,
> In Immanuel's Land.

All heaven revolves round the Christ of Calvary. 'The Lamb as it had been slain', that is, Jesus still bearing the marks of His atoning death, is heaven's temple and light (Rev. 21:22f.) and the focal point of heaven's rule as He occupies His place 'at the centre of the Throne' (Rev. 5:6; 7:17).

There His glory will be displayed in His loving care for His own in the place which He prepared for them at the moment He died for them (John 14:2; Eph. 2:4-6). We shall be for ever with Him (1 Thess. 4:17), and see His face (Rev. 22:4). He will see to it that we are provided for, and will personally superintend our welfare (Rev. 7:17), wiping away every tear so effectually that there will be no more crying, nor even cause to cry (Rev. 21:4). He will take us into such a permanent and secure state that we shall be as 'pillars' in the Temple – permanently secured in Him (Rev. 3:12), and will bestow on us a relation of such intimacy that nothing can describe it but 'the marriage of the Lamb' (Rev. 19:7). Jesus Christ shall indeed be Lord to the glory of God the Father (Phil. 2:11), 'God shall be all in all' (1 Cor. 15:28), and 'there will be no more death' (Rev. 21:4).

8

Snapshots of heaven

The Bible bends down to us in our limitations. God knows that we cannot unloose ourselves from space and time, whether in action or in thought. With perfect grace, therefore, He allows us to think of heaven as a place, and life there as endless time. The reality, of course, will be super-aboundingly, overwhelmingly greater, but here we live with entrancing snapshots.

Philippians: an Overview
There are four references in Philippians which make a convincing bid to summarize heaven, bringing together much of the material we have already harvested in our study.

Bereavement and Sorrow (Phil. 2:27):

> 'God had mercy on him, and not on him only but also on me, to spare me sorrow upon sorrow.'

Life on earth is a mercy of God; to be bereaved of a dear friend is a mountain of heaped-up sorrow.

This is biblical realism. This life is precious to us. It was meant to be so by the will of the Creator (Gen. 2) and even now, though our earthly environment is diminished by sin and we are frustrated and damaged by our sinful natures, life is still precious. And friendships are precious. We love each other and need each other, and to be torn apart is the uttermost earthly sorrow – for even the gentlest death is a cruel cut for the one who is left.

Christians often feel guilty over their tears of bereavement. Sometimes because others force an unreal, non-scriptural triumphalism upon them and they feel that they must 'live up to it'; sometimes because their sensitive spirits tell them that Jesus should be sufficient to dry their tears. Well, so He will (Rev. 7:17), but not yet. In this interim in which He has placed us, His own example at the grave of Lazarus (John 11:35) is our charter and the fact that, as we grow in grace, our emotions become more like His, makes sorrow strike home more sharply and tears flow more readily. Yes, we *are* allowed to weep and He gathers our tears into His bottle (Ps. 56:8).

Striking Camp, Setting Sail (Phil. 1:23):

'I desire to depart and be with Christ.'[1]

Notwithstanding the preciousness of this life, it pales before the prospect of being with Christ. Suppose we know a Christian man who is very ill and we instinctively pray for his recovery: if for a moment we were to think only of him and his personal good (forgetting how dear and necessary he is to his family and the contribution he makes to the Church) – just the person himself – then to pray for his recovery is to pray against his best interests. To die is the last and greatest of God's earthly blessings

---

[1] On *analuo/analusis*, see Chapter 7, Note 5.

because it brings us into a greater fulness of the salvation that is ours in Christ Jesus and, even more, it brings us into the immediate presence of Him who loves us and loosed us from our sins by His blood (Rev. 1:5). Heaven is to be with Jesus.

The Gathered People (Phil. 2:16):

'That I may boast on the day of Christ that I did not run or labour for nothing.'

The word 'boast' grates with us but a paraphrase helps: 'that I may enjoy a real exhilaration of spirit ...'. The thought is striking. When Jesus comes again His glory will capture every eye, His beauty absorb every admiration. The Lamb will be 'all the glory'. Yet, Paul asserts, there would be an exhilaration lacking, a missing dimension, were his Philippians not at his side in that Day.

'Eyes with joy *will* sparkle that brimmed with tears of late – orphans no longer fatherless, nor widows desolate'. There *will* be 'knitting severed friendships where partings are no more'. So Henry Alford put it in his lovely hymn about the 'ten thousand times ten thousand in sparkling raiment bright', but he got his inspiration from the even more glorious Revelation 7:9-17 where 'a huge crowd whom no-one was able to number' drawn from every ethnic group, every tribe, people and language – the blood-bought people – rejoice together, accepted before the throne of God and the Lamb. The roll (Rev. 5:1; 20:15; 21:27) will be called up-yonder and *we* will be there!

Complete at last (Phil. 3:21):

'(He) will transform the bodies of our humiliation that they may become like the body of his glory.'

On earth we determine to begin the day with God, in reading His Word and in prayer, but our bodies keep us late in bed! We long for holiness, but our bodies fight for their less than worthy satisfactions. So what will it be like to have bodies which are themselves adamant for holiness, eager for God? Here and now the battle is unceasing (Rom. 7:7-24) between those aspects of us that are AD and those that are still BC, and the conflict is inescapable (Gal. 5:16-26). Deliverance (Rom. 7:25) is coming but is not yet (Rom. 8:23; 2 Cor. 5:4). Jesus has delivered us from the condemnation of sin, is delivering us from the power of sin and will deliver us from the presence of sin. In that day we shall be like Him for we shall see Him as He is (1 John 3:2).

The marriage

The Throne and the Lamb
In heaven all eyes gaze in one direction. John's description in Revelation 4–5 involves two very homely things. One is that if we come across a group of people all looking in the same direction our automatic reaction is to look in the same direction ourselves; the other is the way our eyes are at first dazzled by sudden light but gradually accustom themselves to it and begin to see clearly. So it was that John, arriving in heaven (4:1), found himself looking at an occupied throne (4:2-3) just because everyone else in the heavenly company was concentrated on the same object (4:4, 6; 5:11). But even though the first light he saw around the throne was that of the rainbow (4:3), the great and gracious sign of the divine covenant of salvation and security (Gen. 9:12-17), yet there was also the brightness of lightning and blazing lamps (4:5). When John's eyes cleared he saw 'a Lamb, looking as if it had been slain, standing in the centre of the throne' (5:6).

In heaven we belong to a Jesus-centred community.

The Lamb who is the Shepherd

The pictures used of the heavenly community, their privileges and their securities, are rich and varied. They are 'at home' with God who 'spreads his tent over them' (Rev. 7:15; contrast Exod. 40:34, 35; see Isa. 4:5); they are provided for and protected (7:16); past sorrows are gone and forgotten (7:17); they have passed into the care of a perfect Shepherd – for who knows better the needs of the sheep than one who is Himself a Lamb (7:17)? The metaphors of the past (Pss. 95:7; 100:3) are the realities of eternity.

In heaven we experience Jesus' shepherding care.

The Marriage of the Lamb

What a daring idea! John Newton wrote of 'Jesus my shepherd, husband, friend, my prophet, priest and king!' but many an editor has felt it right to change 'husband' to 'Saviour' or 'brother'! Yet the Lord Jesus spoke of Himself as the Bridegroom, both present (Mark 2:19) and expected (Matt. 25:1, 6, 10), the King's Son for whom the great wedding feast was prepared (Matt. 22:1). Revelation 19:1-9 takes up this line of truth and once we have accommodated ourselves to the metaphor its meaning is glorious.

In heaven we enjoy permanently the fulness of His love.

The blood of the Lamb

In Revelation the Lord Jesus is pre-eminently the Lamb of God. He is given this lovely title twenty-eight times, almost as frequently as all other names and titles put together.[2] He comes upon the scene as the living Lamb who once was dead (5:6; cf. 1:18) and it is His death that brings the innumerable company into heaven and keeps them safely there. 'They have washed their robes and

---

[2] 'Christ' is used eleven times; 'Jesus' fourteen times; and 'Lord' six times.

made them white in the blood of the Lamb. *Therefore*, they are before the throne of God' (7:14, 15).

'Clothing', of course, as was explained on pages 102-103, is the Bible's way of saying something about the person who wears the clothes. When we are told, therefore, that the heavenly robes are a gift of God (Rev. 6:11), the meaning is that those enjoying heaven have been fitted (and kitted!) for it by God Himself. There is 'oddity' in the claim that a robe washed in blood comes out pure white (7:9, 13-14), but since the robe is a way of saying something about the person who wears it, we know that this washing is to be understood morally and spiritually. The blood of Jesus 'covers' every moral stain and spiritual inadequacy, everything that would of itself unfit us for God and heaven.

This 'covering', however, is not a 'sweeping under the carpet' as though God said of our sins, 'Let's hide them and pretend they are not there.' Rather it is the 'covering' of exact equivalence, as when we say that a certain sum of money will 'cover' a debt. The death of the Lord Jesus exactly covers our debt before the Holy God and so 'covers' us too, like a perfect robe, so that we stand accepted and secure in His presence.

There is also another side to the picture. The white linen of the Bride's dress is 'the righteous acts of the saints' (Rev. 19:8), so that while God provides the robe and Jesus makes it sufficient for heavenly wear, we are called to keep our clothes clean (cf. Rev. 3:4) in readiness to wear them at the great Wedding.

The Holy City: Revelation 21:10–22:5
As we continue this 'refresher course on heaven' there is this great description of the secure and eternal community: the holy city.

We are told seven things about it: It is *God's city*, full of His glory (21:10-11); it is *walled* for security (21:12-13; cf. Gen. 11:1-9) and has strong *foundations* for stability (21:14). These three descriptions (elaborated in 21:15-21) deal with the outward appearance of the city; the remaining four bring us inside: the *temple* (21:22) means that God Himself is actually present in His city; the *light* (21:23) is the glory of Jesus as the Lamb of God; the *people* (21:24-27) are the worldwide people of the Lamb whose names are registered in His book (cf. Rev. 5:1; 20:11-15); and *the life of the city* (22:1-7) is one where everything is new, Eden has been more than restored (22:1, 2; Gen. 2:9, 10-14), the curse lifted (22:3; cf. Gen. 3:14-20) and the Lord present, seen face to face (22:4).

Heaven will be more than we have ever desired, more than a restoration of all that was lost, more indeed than the mind can grasp at present (as the baffling details of the city's dimensions and construction show). But one thing is certain: the city is a perfect revelation and enjoyment of Jesus. There are seven references to Him: His union with His people as *Bridegroom* with Bride, fresh, intimate, permanent (21:9), the *foundation of the truth* which He revealed through His apostles on which the city rests (21:14), the *presence of God* made real in Him (21:22), the *focal point* of the light and glory of God (21:23), the *ground of our citizenship* (21:27), the *source* of our life (22:1), and *the king* under whom we shall reign for ever (22:3, 5).

We will see Him as He is (22:4a) and He will claim and seal us as His own (22:4b).

9

JESUS CHRIST OUR LORD

Death has entered into the experience of God: not at all
the mythical sort of death that ancient peoples used to say
happened annually to their gods, reflecting the death and
life of the annual round of the seasons. No, a real death,
a death that left behind it a body to be buried and a tomb
to be occupied. Of course, as the omniscient God He has
always known all about death but now, in Christ, He has
actually gone through it. We are often perplexed by the
phrase in the Creed which says that 'he descended into
Hell' and would prefer to say what He Himself said that
'He went to Paradise', but let us at least savour the real
comfort it offers: the divine Lord Jesus Christ went through
the whole gamut of death's experiences, including the
transition from this world to the abode of the dead which
the Old Testament called Sheol, the place of the departed.
Richard Baxter put it like this:

> Christ leads me through no darker rooms
> Than he has gone before.

For this reason, we may walk confidently with Christ to meet death. He knows, and He can undertake.

'The Immortal dies'

But how incredible that the Son of God should die! Leave us to the mercies of logic and we must pronounce it the one thing that by definition could not happen. But the Bible tells us that Jesus chose to die, and that it is from His death that the greatest results of all have flowed.

Philippians encloses the whole career of the Lord Jesus in two reflexive verbs, (lit.) 'he emptied himself ... he humbled himself' (2:7, 8). In a voluntarily and self-imposed obedience to the Father's will He laid aside the glories of the heavenly state, and brought His whole divine nature down to earth to live as a man among us; and in the same willing obedience He took the matter one stage further and submitted His immortality to the dominion of death. 'No man takes my life from me': indeed not, for how could anyone take God's life? 'I lay it down of myself' (John 10:18). The Lord Jesus deliberately brought His life to a chosen climax when He gave Himself to die.

More than anything else that He did, His death deserves the title 'The Work of Christ'. It is simply a fact that the New Testament outside the Gospels hardly dwells at all on the works of power He performed, and draws only a few conclusions from the fact that He lived a human life (Heb. 2:17ff.; 4:14ff.), but ever and always returns to His death and itemizes the results that have come from Calvary.

Jesus is Lord

First among these is the lordship of Christ. Whenever we call Him Lord we are looking back to the Cross, 'for to this end Christ died and lived again, that he might be Lord of both the dead the living' (Rom. 14:9). This Lordship came about by a deliberate act of God (Phil. 2:9; Heb. 2:9) as the only fitting return which could be made to Him who carried His obedience to the point of death.

The Servant

Isaiah foresaw this. Predicting the sin-bearing death of the Servant of the Lord, and speaking in the name of God, he said: 'He (the Servant) shall bear their iniquities, therefore will I (God) give him the many as his portion, and he shall take the strong as his spoil' (Isa. 53:12).[1] Note the word 'therefore'. Lordship is the only fitting consequence of the atoning death. Paul took up Isaiah's thought: 'He humbled himself, becoming obedient unto death, even the death of the cross. Wherefore God highly exalted him ... that ... every tongue should confess that Jesus Christ is Lord' (Phil. 2:8, 9).

The whole of heaven, therefore, is a divine reaction to Calvary. We have observed more than once that the central feature of heaven is the enthroned 'Lamb as it had been slain'. This means that the heavenly state is so organized as to express visibly what God thinks of the Cross of Christ. There is no room in this heaven for any new display of divine love. Even heaven itself looks back to the Cross as the one event that gives it all its meaning, purpose and 'shape'. Heaven is balanced – if we may so speak – upon a moment of time, the moment when 'through the eternal Spirit, he offered himself without spot unto God' (Heb. 9:14).

The lordship which Christ exercises in the heavenly places is the lordship of the Lamb of Calvary: a lordship of pure, unutterable benevolence to those who have loved Him (Rev. 7:17), and a lordship of 'the wrath of the Lamb' (Rev. 6:16) to those who have despised the 'one sacrifice for sins for ever' (Heb. 10:12).

Death is vanquished

This lordship cannot be challenged, for, by dying, Jesus has secured for Himself 'the keys of death and of Hades' (Rev. 1:18), that is, complete authority over them, and

---

[1] For this translation of Isaiah 53:12, see Motyer, *Isaiah*, as above.

'being raised from the dead' He 'dies no more; death has no more dominion over him' (Rom. 6:9).

Forces of Evil

We may recall here that death entered the world in the entail of sin. Two coinciding evil forces brought about sin's dominion: on the one hand, the power of Satan, depicted in Genesis as the serpent, the external voice enticing Adam and his wife into sin by specious promises; on the other hand, the power of disobedience, the overthrow of God's appointed order by the rebellion of the human emotions, mind and will (Gen. 3:6).

The New Testament reveals the Cross of Christ as defeating both these forces. As regards Satan, the Son of God came 'to destroy the works of the devil' (1 John 3:8); He Himself predicted that by His Cross 'the prince of this world is cast out' (John 12:31); and the author of Hebrews, looking back to Calvary, teaches that Jesus partook of our flesh and blood 'that through death he might bring to nought him that had the power of death, that is, the devil' (2:14). Calvary was the great single combat between the opposing princes, in which Prince Immanuel triumphed.

As regards the force of Adam's disobedience, which had dragged a whole race, by imputation, into the ruination of sin, the Second Adam, the Lord Jesus, came to counter this by a great act of obedience, and 'as through one man's disobedience the many were made sinners, even so through the obedience of the one shall the many be made righteous' (Rom. 5:19).[2] It was this act of obedience which God rewarded by exalting His son to the highest place which heaven affords.

If we wish to know the certainty of our salvation in Christ, we must dwell upon God's own assessment of the worth of the Cross.

---

[2] J. Murray, *The Imputation of Adam's Sin,* Grand Rapids, 1959; J. R. W. Stott, *The Message of Romans*, IVP, 1994.

Substitution

But however valuable the Cross may appear to God, we need to ask how the death of Christ can have the amazing result of delivering us from death and bringing us to eternal life. What is the relation between Jesus dying on the Cross and the sinners whom He purposed to deliver from death? It is this, that 'by the grace of God he should taste death for every one' (Heb. 2:9). God purposed to 'bring many sons unto glory' (Heb. 2:10), but these are under sentence of death for sin, in bondage to Satan (Heb. 2:14f.) Divine wisdom finds a solution: for every one of them another will 'taste death', that is, experience the death that was properly their due. In other words, He will die in their place.

This substitutionary view of the death of Christ is not peculiar to one passage, but is the uniform teaching of the whole of Scripture as of our Lord Himself when He said that 'the Son of man came not to be ministered unto but to minister, and to give his life a ransom for (instead of) many' (Mark 10:45). Here again are the 'many sons', their lives forfeited to sin and needing to be ransomed; here again is the Son of God bringing them to glory by tasting death in their place, paying out His life instead of theirs.

Simplicity

The simplicity (but a costly simplicity!) of this way of salvation is matched by the simplicity of receiving it: 'Whoever believes in him shall not perish but have everlasting life' (John 3:16).

This whole study has been moving between two opposite eternal destinies: on the one side, the just consequence of sin, the 'perishing' of which this verse speaks; on the other side, the blessed hope of everlasting life. Between these two contrasting states stands the sinner in this life, facing the decision whether to believe in Jesus or to turn away from Him in unbelief. This is the decisive moment.

The act of faith opens the individual life to all the blessings which flow from Calvary because it consists of a trustful repose upon Jesus who alone can save: accepting Him as Saviour and personal commitment unreservedly into His keeping and Lordship. It is the act of one who is enabled by God to say 'Jesus tasted death for me; he is Jesus Christ my Lord.' 'What shall I do to be saved?' asked the jailer at Philippi. Paul's reply is matchless, the glorious simplicity of the gospel: 'Believe in the Lord Jesus and you will be saved' (Acts 16:31).

'So this is Love' (1 John 4:10)
This understanding of the Cross is dominated by appreciation of the love of God and of Jesus for sinners. Love prompted Calvary. 'God commended' – that is, demonstrated, proved and offered – 'his love toward us in that while we were yet sinners Christ died for us' (Rom. 5:8). A more individualistic statement brings home strongly the quality of His love, for 'the Son of God loved me, and gave himself up for me' (Gal. 2:20). Every single sinner whom God purposed to save was personally in the mind of the Saviour, and such was His love that He accepted the task of being the Lamb of God, God's appointed Substitute.

This is more than just the way God loved at a certain moment in the past; it is more than a passing moment of loving concern in the experience of Jesus; this is what love itself is, for 'this is love, not that we loved God but that he loved us and sent his Son to be the propitiation for our sins' (1 John 4:10). There is no other love, no greater love, no coming display of love. The eternal destiny of sinners is settled by personal response to the Christ of Calvary and to the love revealed, defined and offered there. Death is swallowed up by the Cross.[3]

---

[3] S. Motyer, 'Always being given up to Death', *Churchman*, 95.4.81, pp. 294-305.

Bibliography

W. E. Addis etc., *A Catholic Dictionary*, London 1960.

J. N. D. Anderson, *Christianity and World Religions*, IVP, 1984.

B. F. C. Atkinson, *Life and Immortality*, Taunton, 1969.

J. Baillie, *And the Life Everlasting*, OUP, 1961.

E. J. Bicknell, *A Theological Introduction to the Thirty-Nine Articles*, Longman, 1944.

R. P. Blakeney, *The Book of Common Prayer, Its History, and Interpretation*, London 1865.

J. Blanchard, *Whatever Happened to Hell?* Evangelical Press, 1993.

J. Blanchard, *Will the Real Jesus Please Stand Up?* Evangelical Press, 1989.

L. Boettner, *Immortality*, Grand Rapids, 1956.

A. Bonar, *The Book of Leviticus*, Nisbet, 1847.

Book of Common Prayer `

Book of Homilies, Prayer Book Society, 1852.

C. Brown, *Dictionary of New Testament Theology*, Paternoster 1975 etc.

E. Brunner, *Eternal Hope*, Lutterworth, London, 1954.

E. W. Bullinger, *Selected Writings*, Bagster, 1960.

C. S. Carter (and A. Weeks), *The Protestant Dictionary*, Harrison Trust 1933.

Catechism of the Catholic Church, Geoffrey Chapmen, 1995.

H. Constable, *Duration and Nature of Future Punishment*, London, 1886.

O. Cullmann, *Immortality of the Soul or Resurrection of the Body*, London, 1958.

T. Davis, *Endless Suffering Not the Doctrine of Scripture*, Longmans, 1867.

J. Denney, *Studies in Theology*, London, 1894.

R. Dowsett, *God, That's Not Fair!*, IVP, 1985.

D. L. Edwards, *The Last Things Now*, SCM, 1969.

E. E. Ellis, *Paul and his Recent Interpreters*, Grand Rapids, 1961.

A. M. Fairhurst, 'Death and Destiny', *Churchman*, 95/4/1981.

F. W. Farrar, *Eternal Hope*, London 1878.

S. Ferguson, 'Daniel', *New Bible Commentary*, IVP 1994.

L. E. Froom, *Spiritualism Today*, Washington, 1963.

B. Frost, *Some Modern Substitutes for Christianity*, Mowbray, 1942.

W. Fudge, *The Fire That Consumes*, Paternoster, 1994.

N. Geldenhuys, *Commentary on the Gospel of Luke*, Marshall, 1956.

M. Goldsmith, *What about other Faiths?* Hodder and Stoughton, 1989.

E. M. Goulburn, *Everlasting Punishment*, London, 1880.

H. E. Guillebaud, *The Righteous Judge*, Taunton, 1964.

O. Guinness, *The Dust of Death,* IVP, 1973.

D. Guthrie, *The Pastoral Epistles*, IVP, 1957.

D. E. W. Harrison, *The Book of Common Prayer,* London, 1946.

H. C. Hewlett, *The Glories of our Lord*, Ritchie, 1994.

C. Hodge, *Second Corinthians*, Banner of Truth, 1959.

P. E. Hughes, *Paul's Second Epistle to the Corinthians*, Marshall, 1961.

John Paul II, *Lumen Gentium.*

W. Joynson Hicks, *The Prayer Book of Crisis*, Putnam, 1928.

J. N. D. Kelly, *The Pastoral Epistles*, A. & C. Black, 1963.

P. Lewis, *The Glory of Christ*, Hodder and Stoughton, 1992.

H. G. Liddell and R. Scott, *A Greek-English Lexicon*, OUP. 1901.

I. H. Marshall, *The Gospel of Luke*, Paternoster, 1978.

R. Martin-Archard, *From Death to Life*, Oliver and Boyd, 1960.

W. R. Matthews, *The Thirty-Nine Articles*, Hodder and Stoughton, 1961.

W. R. Matthews, *The Hope of Immortality*, Epworth 1966.

J. A. Mohler, *Symbolism, The Doctrinal Differences between Catholics and Protestants*, Catholic Publishing, London, 1843.

L. Morris, *The Wages of Sin*, IVP, 1955.

L. Morris, *The Gospel of Matthew*, IVP, 1992.

J. A. Motyer, 'Psalms', *New Bible Commentary*, IVP, 1994.

J. A. Motyer, *The Prophecy of Isaiah*, IVP, 1993.

J. A. Motyer, *A Scenic Route through the Old Testament*, IVP, 1995.

J. A. Motyer, *Look to the Rock*, IVP, 1996.

S. Motyer, *Remember Jesus*, Christian Focus Publications, 1995.

S. Motyer, 'Always being given up to Death', *Churchman*, 95/4/81.

H. C. G. Moule, *The Second Epistle to Timothy*, RTS, 1905.

J. Murray, *The Imputation of Adam's Sin*, Grand Rapids, 1959.

C. Neil and J. M. Willoughby, *The Tutorial Prayer Book*, Harrison Trust, 1912.

J. I. Packer, *The Problem of Eternal Punishment*, Orthos 1990.

J. B. Payne, *The Theology of the Older Testament*, Zondervan, 1962.

A. Plummer, *The Gospel according to St. Luke*, T. and T. Clark, 1896.

H. Porter, *The Challenge of Spiritualism*, Faith Press, 1938.

E. B. Pusey, *What is of Faith as to Everlasting Punishment?*, OUP. 1880.

J. A. T. Robinson, *In the End, God*, SCM, 1958.

G. Salmon, *The Infallibility of the Church*, Murray 1923.

A. T. Schofield, *Modern Spiritism*, Kessinger Pubs. 2003.

E. K. Simpson, *The Pastoral Epistles*, IVP, 1954.

J. P. Smyth, *The Gospel of the Hereafter*, London 1964.

A. M. Stibbs, *The Finished Work of Christ*, IVP, 1954.

J. R. W. Stott, *Christ the Controversialist*, IVP, 1970.

J. R. W. Stott, *The Cross of Christ*, IVP, 1986.

J. R. W. Stott, *The Message of Romans*, IVP, 1994.

J. R. W. Stott and D. L. Edwards, *Essentials, A Liberal-Evangelical Dialogue*, Hodder & Stoughton, 1988.

S. W. Sykes, 'Death and Doctrine', *Churchman*, 95/4/81.

S. Travis, *Christian Hope and the Future of Man*, IVP, 1981.

R. V. G. Tasker, *The Gospel according to John*, IVP, 1960.

R. C. Trench, *Synonyms of the New Testament*, Paul Trench, 1894.

J. von Baalen, *The Chaos of the Cults*, Grand Rapids, 1948.

G. von Rad, *Old Testament Theology*, SCM, 1962, 1965.

Th. C. Vreizen, *An Outline of Old Testament Theology*, Blackwell, 1960.

J. Waterworth, *The Canons and Decrees of the Council of Trent*, London 1848.

J. W. Wenham, *The Case for Conditional Immortality*, Rutherford House 1991.

J. S. Wright, 'The Supposed Evidence for Reincarnation', *Journal of the Transactions of the Victoria Institute*, Vol. LXXXIII, 1951.

J. S. Wright and J. O. Sanders, *Some Modern Religions*, IVP 1956.

N. T. Wright, *Who was Jesus?* SPCK, 1992.

N. T. Wright, *For All The Saints: Remembering the Christian Departed*, SPCK, 2003,

TRUTHFORLIFE®

Truth For Life is the Bible-teaching ministry of Alistair Begg. Our mission is to teach the Bible with clarity and relevance so that unbelievers will be converted, believers will be established, and local churches will be strengthened.

Since 1995, Truth For Life has aired a Bible-teaching program on the radio, which is now distributed on 1,667 radio outlets each day, and freely on podcast and on the Truth For Life mobile app. Additionally, a large content archive of full-length Bible-teaching sermons is available for free download at www.truthforlife.org.

Truth For Life also makes full-length Bible-teaching available on CD and DVD. These materials, and also books authored by Alistair Begg, are made available at cost, with no markup, so that price is not a barrier to those seeking a deeper understanding of God's Word.

The ministry connects with listeners at live listener and pastor events and conferences across the U.S. and Canada in cities where the radio program is heard.

Contact Truth For Life

In the U.S.:
PO Box 398000, Cleveland, OH 44139, 1.888.588.7884
www.truthforlife.org   letters@truthforlife.org

In Canada:
P.O. Box 19008, Delta, BC V4L 2P8, 1.877.518.7884
www.truthforlife.ca   letters@truthforlife.ca

And also at:
www.facebook.com/truthforlife   www.twitter.com/truthforlife

Christian Focus Publications

Our mission statement –

STAYING FAITHFUL

In dependence upon God we seek to impact the world through literature faithful to His infallible Word, the Bible. Our aim is to ensure that the Lord Jesus Christ is presented as the only hope to obtain forgiveness of sin, live a useful life and look forward to heaven with Him.

Our Books are published in four imprints:

CHRISTIAN FOCUS

popular works including biographies, commentaries, basic doctrine and Christian living.

CHRISTIAN HERITAGE

books representing some of the best material from the rich heritage of the church.

MENTOR

books written at a level suitable for Bible College and seminary students, pastors, and other serious readers. The imprint includes commentaries, doctrinal studies, examination of current issues and church history.

CF4•K

children's books for quality Bible teaching and for all age groups: Sunday school curriculum, puzzle and activity books; personal and family devotional titles, biographies and inspirational stories – Because you are never too young to know Jesus!

Christian Focus Publications Ltd,
Geanies House, Fearn, Ross-shire,
IV20 1TW, Scotland, United Kingdom.
www.christianfocus.com